Family Reins

BILLY BUSCH

THE EXTRAORDINARY RISE AND EPIC FALL
OF AN AMERICAN DYNASTY

**BLACK
STONE**
PUBLISHING

Printed in the United States of America

First edition: 2023
ISBN 979-8-200-79882-7
Biography & Autobiography / Business

Version 1

Blackstone Publishing
31 Mistletoe Rd.
Ashland, OR 97520

www.BlackstonePublishing.com

*This book is dedicated to my wife, Christi,
who inspires me to do better and be better each day.
And to my seven beautiful children, I hope you can understand me a little
better and in turn understand your legacy.*

Contents

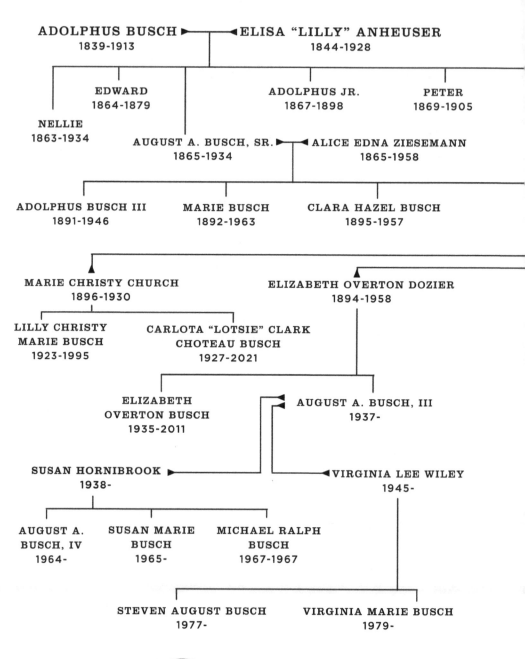

ADOLPHUS BUSCH ► ◄ **ELISA "LILLY" ANHEUSER**
1839-1913   1844-1928

EDWARD
1864-1879

ADOLPHUS JR.
1867-1898

PETER
1869-1905

NELLIE
1863-1934

AUGUST A. BUSCH, SR. ► ◄ **ALICE EDNA ZIESEMANN**
1865-1934   1865-1958

ADOLPHUS BUSCH III
1891-1946

MARIE BUSCH
1892-1963

CLARA HAZEL BUSCH
1895-1957

MARIE CHRISTY CHURCH
1896-1930

ELIZABETH OVERTON DOZIER
1894-1958

LILLY CHRISTY MARIE BUSCH
1923-1995

CARLOTA "LOTSIE" CLARK CHOTEAU BUSCH
1927-2021

ELIZABETH OVERTON BUSCH
1935-2011

AUGUST A. BUSCH, III
1937-

SUSAN HORNIBROOK ►
1938-

◄ **VIRGINIA LEE WILEY**
1945-

AUGUST A. BUSCH, IV
1964-

SUSAN MARIE BUSCH
1965-

MICHAEL RALPH BUSCH
1967-1967

STEVEN AUGUST BUSCH
1977-

VIRGINIA MARIE BUSCH
1979-

Busch

F A M I L Y   T R E E

FOLLOWING THE LINEAGE OF WILLIAM KURT BUSCH

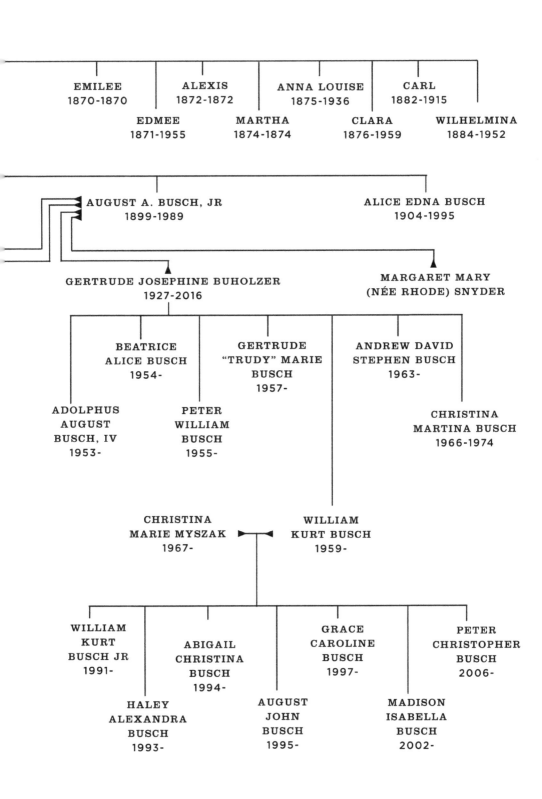

Prologue

The bell rings out. We can hear it from every single spot on the 281 acres of the farm. It's as if all of South St. Louis can hear it. My siblings and I know what to do. We have to stop everything and head back to the house. There isn't a good excuse if we don't make it back to the house in time. By the time the second bell goes off, we best be on our way.

Dad is coming home.

Several minutes later, I hear Dad laying on the loud musical horn of his brown Mercedes 500 sedan as he makes his way up the long drive to our house. It is the golden hour. The sun is beginning to lower in the sky, casting a warm glow over the grounds, which are showing the premature signs of autumn as the heat of the August day wanes and burns off. The maples are highlighted with a bit of yellow, not yet the bright orange they will ultimately turn in the weeks to come. The tips of the oak leaves are beginning to brown, and the sweet smell of decaying leaves tinges the heavy, humid late-summer air. As I run back to the house to change my shirt and make myself presentable, the prematurely fallen leaves crunch beneath me.

My father's horn blares again, and the elk bugle in the Deer Park as if they, too, are his royal subjects, announcing the sounds of his arrival in response. *Da-da-da-da-dun-da-da-da!* The King of Beers returning to his throne. He has spent the day working at the brewery and now is his time to shine. *All hail the King of Beers*, the sound seems to say, and instantly, all around us, the property transforms.

Visitors seem to straighten up and begin to rush from wherever they are, hoping to get a glimpse of Dad and perhaps a photo for their scrapbooks. The throngs form from all points on the property—the trams that cart them through the grounds; the petting zoo; the goat pen; the milk house; outside the kangaroo corral and the elephant, lemur, camel, llama, and alpaca enclosures; next to the Five Fountain Lake area; in the biergartens; and from President Grant's hand-hewn wood cabin.

Workers hustle to put their final touches on the day. In the concession stands, servers make sure the Budweiser taps are running fresh and cold. Groundskeepers scurry around, raking and sweeping. They are careful that not so much as a single leaf or branch is out of place. Maintenance crews walk through the grounds and look for any errant pieces of trash—beer cups that missed their mark in the garbage cans or field trip name tags that came loose and landed in the beautifully manicured garden beds. Grooms pull the horses from their stables. The horses are fed, watered, brushed, dressed, and ready to go. The coach has already been pulled from one of the fifty carriage displays and is polished, ready, and waiting for Dad's arrival and inspection. The stable hands walk around it one last time, scrutinizing every detail—its red-spoked wheels, its black upholstered seat, its leather reins. Everything has to be perfect.

My mother, who has spent the afternoon preening for the moment of Dad's arrival, emerges from the Big House dressed to the nines, as always, albeit appropriately so for her daily ride on the coach through the grounds with my father. For these rides, she wears her custom-made leather riding boots, camel-colored riding pants, and a crisp white cotton button-down shirt. Her blond hair, cut in the style of Jackie Kennedy and curling just at her chin, is perfectly coiffed. Not one hair is out of place. She wears no makeup and, truthfully, doesn't need to. She sleeps nearly twelve hours a night, waking late in the day, in order to keep her skin youthful and glowing. By all accounts, she is picture perfect, the epitome of class and elegance. As the horn gets louder, she makes her way to greet my father, waving and smiling to her subjects.

I run to Yolanda, my nurse (the European term for a nanny). I also have to look sharp for my father. Yolanda hurries to comb my blond hair properly. Since I am running late already and am not too dirty from the day's events, the only thing she makes me change is my shirt. I do so quickly. A sharp white shirt has already been laid out and pressed for me. Thankfully, I don't have to change out of the rolled-up jeans and cowboy boots, which I wore all day. As long as I am not covered in mud or animal feces, I am permitted to keep the jeans and boots on. I am allowed this small concession. It's not always a guarantee.

On most summer days, while my mom is sleeping and Dad is at the brewery, I am free to run around with my pet turkey, Black Radish. Some days I help feed and care for the animals. On others, I explore the park or work the concessions, serving visitors and passing out food and beer, or head over to the carpenter shop and help out there. When we're feeling up to a little adventure, sometimes my siblings and I go to the hayloft and swing on the ropes or head over to the goat house and ride the sheep, pretending they're bulls. On hot days, we spend the afternoon in the kidney-shaped swimming pool. Whenever we want to get from one point to the other, we jump on the back of the moving trams that cart public visitors and onlookers throughout the property.

Some days I hide, hoping to get out of the ritual. But today I have been "seen" and hand-selected. My mother specifically requested I, her eight-year-old husky cherub of a son, ride with her and my dad. So I have to be ready to go or suffer her wrath.

When I am deemed presentable, Yolanda sends me on my way.

"You better take the car or you'll be late," she recommends.

I nod. I know how disrespectful it is to be late.

I rush through the house, which seems to take forever. That is, of course, because the "house" is, by most people's standards, more like a castle. Built in the design of a French Renaissance château, it boasts thirty-four rooms and has a beautiful, red-tiled mansard roof. The massive front door sits right in the center of a nearly one hundred-yard-long grand portico lined with a limestone railing and outfitted with large stone flowerpots overflowing with petunias and ivy. The brick-and-limestone exterior of the house reaches four stories high and showcases intricately hand-carved dormer windows that jut out from the cornice-trimmed roofline. The enormous building is flanked on either side by large turrets topped with pointy aged-copper finials—a finishing touch that makes it look every bit like a Bavarian castle one might find in a Disney movie. A stranger looking upon it might assume it's a home fit for a king that one might tour while on trips through the German countryside. But no, behind the turrets and forty-five large windows that span the width of its front, lives the Busch family: my dad, his third wife, and his seven kids from their marriage. His older children from his previous marriages live elsewhere now, though at one point they, too, were raised here.

I run across the massive expanse of manicured lawn that surrounds the house, passing our swimming pool, pond, and family chapel—a gift to my mother on the occasion of my birth and where we attend a private Mass every Sunday. Beyond, the "yard" that surrounds the house is more of an amusement park / zoo / biergarten / nature preserve / national historic site.

The final bell rings. It's so loud, I feel it in my bones.

My childhood is punctuated by bells, horns, and the noise made by hundreds of workers. Some of these sounds occur just outside my bedroom window first thing in the morning—lawns being mowed and grounds being maintained—while others are more distant—donkeys braying, horses neighing, gibbon monkeys howling, elephants calling out to each other, and the guides on the trams describing each location as they carry visitors onto our property.

"Here, if you look closely, you can catch a glimpse of the Busches' private residence," the guides explain. "Grant's Farm, the Anheuser-Busch family estate, was purchased in 1907 by August Sr., father of the current owner and president of Anheuser-Busch, Gussie Busch. Prior to the Busch family owning the property, the 281-acre estate was originally the location of President Ulysses S. Grant's first home, a cabin that he built for his wife, Julia Dent, on the eighty acres her father bequeathed to them as a wedding present, which we'll be headed to shortly . . ." The guides' voices trail off as the trams move through the grounds.

Since I am running late on this particular day, I take Yolanda's advice and hop into my miniature motorcar—much like the ones you might actually see in Disneyland. The one I drive, however, isn't attached to rails. Even at eight years old, I am an experienced driver. I speed through the park and make my way up to the *Bauernhof*, a massive courtyard built to replicate nineteenth-century Bavarian farms—complete with a clock tower, stables, a fifty-space carriage house, and quarters for those who live and work there. Our Bauernhof features a world-renowned carriage collection and stables filled with some of the most beautiful horses in the world, most notably our iconic Clydesdales, as well as the stately Hackneys and world-class hunters and jumpers.

I am barely on time. Dad, a man who loves to make an entrance, pulls into the courtyard of the grand space just after I do. The workers quickly step in front of his car to help part the crowd that surrounds him, cheering him and screaming his name: *Hey Gussie! Hey Gussie! Mr. Busch! Hey Mr. Busch!*

He eats it up. And so do I. He's my dad after all. And he makes for quite the show.

My mother emerges and greets my father, and together they wave to the crowd as they make their way across the courtyard to the coach, which has been prepared for us. The farm manager, who regularly meets my father upon his arrival, follows along as Dad looks the carriage over: pulling the reins, inspecting the horses, checking the wheels. No detail is too small. Dad doesn't miss a thing. When he's satisfied, he pulls out a cigarette and takes a drag, careful not to blow smoke in the animals' faces. He's a gentleman after all.

One stableman greets him and gives him his riding apron and gloves, another takes his jacket and tie. My father wraps the apron around himself and pulls the gloves on. I am standing close enough to him that

I can smell his signature scent: St. John's Bay Rum cologne, a blend of eucalyptus, cloves, a variety of Caribbean spices, and a hint of cinnamon. His salt-and-pepper hair also has a distinct scent; he wears it slicked back with the help of Vitalis. Always self-conscious about how his breath smells as a smoker, he pulls out a tin of tiny black licorice squares, Sen-Sens, and pops one in his mouth.

"Ready to go, Billy the Kid?" he asks.

I nod expectantly.

My father adjusts his gloves and apron. Like my mother, my father appreciates a put-together look. Though my mother is understated—never painting her nails or wearing too much jewelry—my father loves a little glitz. He wears Gucci loafers and leaves the house each day festooned in a gold watch and gold rings, bracelets, and necklaces. Everywhere the sun touches him, he sparkles—his hair, his ruddy cheeks, his wrists, and his fingers. And just as his physical presence emanates light, so does his charismatic and gregarious personality. He has an easy smile and chats up everyone who works for him. Even over the loud bustling noises of the crowds, I can make out Dad's raspy voice, delivering instructions, catching up with workers, and dropping the one-liner jokes he's so famous for. He loves to greet people with a hearty laugh and, "So, when did you get out of jail?"

After he's finished making the rounds, another of the stable hands pulls the ladder aside the carriage and guides my mother up. I follow suit. Finally, my father joins us and takes the reins in his gloved hands.

"Hey, pal," he says again, acknowledging my presence.

"Hey, Dad," I say back, knowing not to say anything else unless explicitly asked.

The farm manager finally ascends and takes his place in back of us. He is here to take mental notes. As my father rides through the grounds, he'll be giving instructions about what needs to be fixed, what needs to be cleaned up, and what animals need to be attended to or taken to the vet to be treated. As much as the crowd thinks this is a pleasant family joyride, it's still very much part of my father's workday.

But it's not work for me. Even though on some days I would indeed

dread it, mainly because I hated to be pulled away from my beloved animals to get cleaned up and sit between my two parents, once we are on
our way, it is an absolute thrill.

The stable workers and maintenance crews again help part the crowd
that cheer us as we make our way out of the Bauernhof and into the
park. My father is a great whip. I can hear the *clip-clop, clip-clop* of the
horses' feet as they move together in tandem. As we travel through the
park, more visitors come and wave and cheer, and my mother, as if she
were the Queen herself, waves back, clearly in her element. Swiss born
and raised, she loves the great outdoors, and she adores the farm. She
equally adores being the center of attention. These rides are the high-
light of her day.

"Isn't it just lovely, dahhhling?" she says in her strong Swiss accent,
accentuating the *ahh* in *darling* and emphasizing the hard *g* sound at
the end, like a true lady of elegance.

This comment I know is directed at me, and I also know my job
is simply to agree, which isn't hard to do. It is lovely. It's downright
beautiful.

Being out on the coach next to my father, who is nearly thirty years
older than my mother and the age of most of my friends' grandparents,
is truly a special occasion. By the time the seven of us kids came along,
he was already getting on in age. He is also at the height of his career—
running the world's largest brewery, opening several amusement parks,
and owning the St. Louis Cardinals. When he isn't working at the brewery or traveling around the country in our family's private railcar visiting
his distributorships, he and my mother are entertaining. The only time
we have our parents to ourselves is over dinner in the evening, during
which we listen to them talk about the brewery, while under the watch-
ful eye of our servants and nannies. To be able to sit between them on a
carriage and have them (almost) all to myself is a rare and special treat.

Once we are out of view of the visitors and inaccessible to the public,
it is as if we really are a family and no longer a circus act. My dad begins
to relax. I can almost feel him exhale all the stress of the day along with
the smoke from his Marlboro Reds. My mother, on the other hand,

never seems to cast off her regal air, no matter where we are, although, depending on the day, she certainly appreciates the time outside alone with my father and one or more of her children.

Occasionally, in between his directives to the farm manager and speaking to my mother in German—so no one else can understand what they are saying, including me—he asks me what I did on the farm that day. He looks me in the eye as he speaks, something he values. Truly, I am amazed by this, since he can carry on conversations at the same time that he can control four horses perfectly.

I don't dare tell him how I sampled chewing tobacco for the first time that day with some farmhands and got so dizzy, I drove my car off the road. There are some secrets I know to keep to myself. So, I give him a brief update about the baby elephants in my care. I tell him how I brought them up to the fence to greet the public. I look up for his approval and he nods. He wants his kids to be comfortable with the public. After all, "Making friends is our business" is the family and company motto.

I then tell him about the antics of the miniature horse we recently acquired.

He laughs.

Following his lead, I do too.

I tell him about the baby bears, and how they got away from us and ran up a tree that I had to climb to get them back. And I tell him about the baby camels and baby llamas and all the babies that arrived earlier in the spring.

He asks me if I did any "real work." Being eight years old is no excuse for a Busch family member not to work.

"Yes, sir, I helped sell milk bottles today and worked the concession stand with Adolphus."

He does not ask me how I am feeling. He doesn't ask me who I played with. He isn't concerned about whether I read books over the summer or if I am participating in club or team sports (which I am not). He is concerned only with the farm and what my role on the farm is. I know my place and I take it. When he is done with his questioning, I don't offer any other details. I simply sit, listen, and watch. Instinctively, like the horses in front of me, I let my father lead. I take my cues from him. My job is to learn from the master. Where he directs the reins, I go.

As we crest the hill and overlook the farm, the hides of the horses begin to glisten. The evening sun, though less intense, is still hot, and so my father directs the coach off to the shade to let the animals rest for a bit. We, too, sit in the shade and enjoy the rare and peaceful moment, where my father is the king of his castle, my mother the queen of everything, and I—his pal, his son—am sitting there right between them both. There is nothing to do. Nothing to clean up. Nothing to fix. And for an ephemeral moment, my father and I are so close and so connected I can almost feel what he is feeling. We're both marveling at the life we've been born into, a life that I know few people other than my siblings will ever be able to say they have lived, a life he has worked his ass off day and night to provide for me—for all of us.

Of course, I have no way of knowing that as we sit under the tree and watch the sun setting over his kingdom, that the steady hands that just deftly guided our horses into shade that evening, the hands that have so capably held the family reins, would soon lose their grip. Nor have I any idea that in the decades that lie ahead, everything we know, everything we enjoyed, everything our ancestors bequeathed to us, would be undone. This farm, this fairy-tale life, would become nothing but a memory for me that would ring through my heart, like a bell calling me home.

Part One

WHAT WOULD ADOLPHUS DO?

Chapter One
THE KING OF BEERS

When you live in a fairy tale, it's easy to assume that it has always been and always will be magical. There is no sense that there was a "before" or that there could ever be "The End."

I grew up in such a surreal existence, I now realize. Of course, at five, eight, ten years old, I had no idea that my childhood was different from most. I also realize that being a Busch child was very different from being a Busch adult. Back then I didn't know what was going on behind the scenes or what had gone on long before I arrived to make all of this "magic" happen.

It wasn't until I was in my forties—with children of my own—that it began to hit me how little I knew about the true and whole history of the Busch family—the improbability of the inception of it, and the struggles to survive over nearly two centuries and several generations, from my great-grandfather Adolphus to my grandfather August Sr. and then to his heirs who led the company after his death: my uncle Adolphus III and then, of course, my father, August Jr., "Gussie."

As an adult Busch, I worked on the grounds of Grant's Farm, then in the distributorships, and even played polo for the Bud Light team. My life was so thoroughly "Busch" I never saw the need to stop and think about how it all started or that it ever might end—that the reins that held us together were loosening and might break away al-together. I had no idea how fragile it had been in so many ways. On paper we Busch heirs are listed as being worth more than $13 billion combined. According to *Forbes*, we're one of the twenty richest fam-ilies in America. We've been an American staple since 1876—and I'm not just talking about our beer. Our family, our advertising—especially our iconic Clydesdales—and our style of business have all become synonymous with *America*. We're the poster children of the American dream—that not-so-outdated belief that hard work, entre-preneurship, grit, and a positive can-do attitude can make anything possible. From the company's inception, Adolphus was committed to passing that belief onto his son and was hell-bent on keeping it within the family forever. This tradition reigned supreme. *It was a family busi-ness. End of story.* Back then everyone chipped in, and everyone did their part to help the company. As much as I was born into a family, I was also born into a business. There was never supposed to be a separation—ever. This we knew. This was our legacy. My father wasn't just my father. He was my boss. He told us what to do, and we did it. We were all there to help out. I didn't know where my family ended and the business started. They were so closely entangled that it lives that way in my memories too.

One of the biggest regrets of my life, and why I have so thoroughly dedicated my life to my children, is that I never truly got to know my father—*as my father.* Sure, I spent time with him. I sat beside him while he took the reins and inspected the park. When I was very young, we traveled with him, as he did with his father and grandfather, by private railcar. As I got older, we cut the travel time down to our home in St. Petersburg, Florida, from two days to four hours when we traveled via the private two-propeller Gulfstream. By the time I was in my early teens, it only took us a couple of hours to get to Florida in the private jet. Although, that's not the only way we got around—I recall traveling aboard my father's 120-foot-long yacht—the famous *A & Eagle.* We usu-ally boarded it from our compound on the bay of St. Petersburg, where we docked our yachts and fishing and recreational boats. Here we also owned several houses where our housekeepers, chef, butlers, chauffeurs, and some company employees stayed.

The family lived on the beachside of St. Petersburg in a spacious house with seven bedrooms that overlooked the Gulf of Mexico. It was where, over the years, my father entertained the Cardinals baseball team, baseball Hall of Famers, and many sports greats such as Jack Buck, Lou Brock, Stan Musial, Mike Shannon, Bob Gibson, Harry Caray, Ozzie Smith, Pete Rose, and Marge Schott. He also hosted many dignitaries and celebrities at home and on the yacht, such as Ed McMahon and Ulysses S. Grant III, the president's grandson.

In 1975 we took the *A & Eagle* up the coast of Florida to Williamsburg, Virginia. We sailed right up the James River and pulled into the newly acquired land my father had bought from Colonial Williamsburg and turned into a brewery and family-attraction theme park. He had hoped it would help bring tourism and more jobs to the area. I don't know many kids who can say they arrived to spend a day at a theme park *that their father owned* by way of a yacht. It was memorable even for me, who, in so many ways, took for granted the ease with which we traveled back then. And yet, we had lots of routine outings too—like attending Cardinals baseball games in Busch Stadium.

My father lived for the company—and all that it entailed. It was all he thought about, talked about, and gave his energy to. I sat with him at the dinner table each night and listened (we spoke only when spoken to) as he and my mother discussed that day's work in the brewery. He didn't have much time for us kids. And there were a lot of us—seven from his marriage with my mother, Trudy, (Adolphus IV, Beatrice, Peter, Gertrude, Andrew, Christina, and of course, me) and four from his two previous marriages (Lilly and Lotsie from his first marriage, and Elizabeth and August III from his second). Of course, by the time I came along, most of the older children were either long gone or so much older than me, they were practically strangers—or at the very least like cousins or aunts or uncles. In fact, because of the age difference, though we knew they were our half siblings, my father and mother requested we call Lotsie, Lilly, Elizabeth, and August III, as well as all adults, by the formal *Aunt* or *Uncle*. Though kids of the current generation may not be familiar with this notion, it was a form of endearment and respect, and my parents expected us to treat our elders with the utmost respect.

My father left the rearing of us seven children to my mother, who in turn left it to the cadre of servants, housekeepers, gardeners, chauffeurs, nannies, farmhands, and cooks as she readied herself for my father each day with her own team: a hairdresser and manicurist. Now, I know he loved us—there is no doubt or question about that—but my father wasn't a man who spoke the words specifically or regularly. He wasn't a man who knew each one of his kids, at least not in the way I know my own. I certainly couldn't imagine speaking to my father the way my wife, Christi, talks to her parents or my children talk to me—so freely and openly.

While many people have come to know Christi and my children through our MTV reality show, *The Busch Family Brewed*, there are so many more stories that people don't know, conversations they don't see when the cameras aren't rolling. My wife and I take parenting very seriously. It's the most important job we'll ever have. There is something so amazing about parenting and fatherhood. I never take it for granted. When I held my firstborn, Billy Jr., in my arms, I promised him I would get to know him—all of my children—in a way my father never knew me. I also wanted to be able to share with them parts of my life and growing up, because I never had that kind of relationship with my own dad. Through the years I have passed on some of these stories, but in so many ways this book is for them so that they will know the history too. So that they will know the legacy they have inherited the way I know it, respect it, and revere it. I want them to know their father in a way I never got to know my own.

That being said, for all that talk of not "knowing" or "getting deep" with my dad, I was *there*. I saw him in action. What I knew about growing up an heir to the Busch family I learned from the front row—sitting at the dinner table beside my father, living in his home. My siblings and

I are the few people in the world who saw firsthand what being a Busch meant to him. Just as my father grew up in the brewery and personally watched his father, August Sr., run the company during some of the most tumultuous times for this country and the brewery. Though I was not privy to what was happening behind closed doors at the brewery—only what he said about the day's events after the fact. I witnessed how the work energized him, gave him purpose, joy, and something to fight and live for. I also saw how tightly he held onto it, how he reacted and spiraled when it slipped from his grasp, and how strongly he railed against the injustice of it all being taken away from him so cruelly in the end.

He made me pick a side when things started to sour. The ultimatum from him was clear: *It's them or me.* In the end, I chose my father. I chose him not because I knew what was right for the company or what was going on, but out of loyalty and love. He was my hero. My shining beacon in the darkest night. But like a beacon, he stood alone, far from me—from so many people. We could see his light, but we could not penetrate the fortress beneath. We could not know the depth of his personal hell or the pain he was going through. In truth, I never tried. We didn't have that type of relationship. It was a relationship of smart quips, jabs to the shoulder, bonding over sports and company talk, and short sayings. It was common for my siblings and me to hear him ask rhetorically: "What would Adolphus do?" There was no need to reply. The answer resided in the history, the myth, the legacy that was our family lore. It was shorthand for a laundry list of values and behaviors that drove the Busch family to success.

In 2006 my kids were getting older, I knew my time playing polo competitively was running out, and I was thinking about going back into running a distributorship myself. So I finally sat down and read *Making Friends Is Our Business: 100 Years of Anheuser-Busch*, the definitive history written in 1953 by Roland Krebs and Percy J. Orthwein. I was just in awe of the incredible effort that it took my great-grandfather, grandfather, and father to build the family business. This led me to explore all the photo albums, notes, and memorabilia my father had collected over the years.

Christi and I would get lost for hours poring over letters he wrote. I had known my father as an older man, but the letters that he wrote as a young man to his wife showed a romantic and sentimental side to him I rarely, if ever, saw. Through piles and piles of letters, notes, even cocktail napkins and matchboxes he collected from events over the years, Christi and I were able to piece together the story of his childhood; his relationships with his parents, his grandfather Adolphus, his wives, and his children; and ultimately what really mattered to him. We got to know the man in a way we couldn't while he was alive. I couldn't believe I didn't know any of this when I was a boy—that my father didn't share these stories with me. I suppose it was because we were too busy at the time making our own.

Sure, I had heard the family legends. The most poignant is the one where my great-grandfather Adolphus and his brewmaster, Carl Conrad, traveled to Germany, trying to come up with the idea for the perfect beer. They went everywhere trying different beers. Then one evening they had trouble finding a place to sleep. They were exhausted after a night of riding horses through town after town when they ended up in a small bohemian town called Budweis. As if this story wasn't biblical enough, there was "no room at the inn" for the poor fellows, but they found a light shining outside the door of a Benedictine monastery. The porter who met them said that they could come in but would need to wait to sleep. The monks were just gathering for dinner, and they invited the men to join them. The two exhausted travelers sat down to a meal, which was, of course, served with the monks' homemade brew. Adolphus and Carl took their first sip and fell instantly in love. They asked the monks to show them how they made it. That recipe became the legendary King of Beers, Budweiser. The rest is history.

These were the types of stories I heard as a boy—part magic, part legend. And it's a great story. Whether it was 100 percent true or not didn't matter to me back then. I don't even remember the moment I heard it for the first time. Memories are fleeting, like dreams to me now. It was passed around so much—and of course, over time liberties were taken with a detail here and there, as stories and memories are wont to do.

The boy who grew up into a man and then became a father became more interested in true stories. The fairy-tale version had been smashed long before that, and I wasn't interested in legends anymore. I'd had my fill of those. I wanted to know the truth. I wanted to understand my father and what made him the man he was, what made my siblings the way they were, and what ultimately tore us all apart. I also wanted to know how to start a business of my own and carry on the family legacy my ancestors and father fought so mightily for and which this current generation lost.

I never met my great-grandfather Adolphus Busch, yet his memory loomed large because he so deeply lived in my father. Most of us who grew up with living grandparents know what a strong and lifelong impression they can leave on a grandchild's heart and mind. My father was a teenager when Adolphus died. He was there when his grandfather, beloved in St. Louis, arrived back from his vacation home in Germany in a casket and was paraded through the streets of St. Louis like the war hero he was (Civil War, that is).

I wanted to *know* Adolphus myself. I figured that if I could understand him better, I could see things more clearly and perhaps be in a better position to change some of the outcomes for my own children. We are very much a result of our pasts and our legacies, but I also believe that we can learn from past mistakes and create a better future for ourselves and future generations.

Through reading *Making Friends Is Our Business* and the memorabilia my father left behind, I found out that my great-grandfather arrived in America in 1857 at just eighteen years old—along with a million German immigrants in that decade. Adolphus's ship arrived at the port of New Orleans. He wasn't poor—by any stretch. He was the second-to-last of twenty-two children born to a wealthy wine merchant and, like many Germans, was seeking to build even more fortune in the free market of the great idea that was the United States of America. With more than a quarter of St. Louis's inhabitants being German, Adolphus knew that St. Louis would be the best spot for him to get his start. He had already heard that he would have no problem securing work there.

The place was teeming with breweries, cultural venues, German places of worship, and even German newspapers.

He traveled up the mighty Mississippi and hopped off the riverboat wide-eyed, his heart filled with possibility. I can only imagine the sights he must have seen. There was no iconic arch back then or steel bridges crossing the river's mighty expanse. There were no skyscrapers or casinos along the shoreline. Yet St. Louis was still a bustling industrious city for its time and brimming with promise. Adolphus wasted no time getting started.

As a son of a wealthy businessman involved in numerous undertakings, Adolphus had a businessman's mind. He knew where to seek out opportunities by identifying what customers needed. There were already many breweries in St. Louis. What the area needed was a supply company. It just made sense. He worked for two years as a riverboat clerk, making friends and getting connected while planning and saving for the right move. When his father passed away in 1859, he used his inheritance to buy into an already established supply company, which he renamed the Wattenberg, Busch & Company—and quickly began expanding his business. It became one of the most successful wholesale houses in St. Louis.

One of his repeat customers was Eberhard Anheuser, another wealthy businessman who was trying to turn around a failing brewery and make it profitable. At some point in their growing business relationship and friendship, no doubt at one of the many social events and parties, Eberhard introduced his daughter Lilly to Adolphus. The two married on March 7, 1861.

Not long after they married, the South seceded from the Union and America was at war. Though my great-grandfather had only been in the country for eight years, he felt the desire to support the Union, and so he joined the fight.

When he returned from the war, he found out that his father-in-law's brewery had racked up a large amount of debt. The crux of the issue was that he brewed terrible beer and the discerning St. Louis patrons had their pick of fine-tasting beers throughout the city.

Adolphus offered to help his father-in-law and began working for him. He split his time working at the brewery and the supply company until 1869 when he sold his interest in Wattenberg, Busch & Company to devote all his time to brewery operations. Despite the less-than-stellar recipe, Adolphus somehow managed to turn the company around, and in 1873, Lilly's father made Adolphus a partner. Adolphus owned a minority stake, but when Eberhard died in 1880, Lilly's inherited shares were added to Adolphus's and that gave him the majority stake in the company, which was renamed the Anheuser-Busch Brewing Association. He was now the first Busch to be president of Anheuser-Busch.

Adolphus's first move was to change that awful recipe. He knew it wouldn't be difficult to sell a great-tasting beer. He traveled through Europe in search of the perfect recipe (which he found in the town of Budweis), then partnered with his friend Carl Conrad to establish the Budweiser brand. There's always a bit of truth in every legend, isn't there?

Now that he had a great sales strategy (he made friends with everyone) and the greatest, smoothest-tasting pale lager in town, he could begin to grow his budding business.

My great-grandfather was not a contented man. Contented men rarely seek out innovative ideas. In contrast, he was always on the vanguard of what was new and groundbreaking and was always trying to find ways to edge out the competition. He was the first brewer to pasteurize beer. This allowed him to bottle and store the beer, without fear of it spoiling. As his production sped up and they were capable of making large quantities that lasted for longer periods, he thought it would be advantageous to set up a system of railside icehouses so that his beer could go anywhere trains went. He became the first brewer to set up national distribution.

Looking for ways to improve icehouses, he was also the first brewer to use artificial (non-ice) refrigeration. He first used it in his plant and then began to outfit train cars with it so beer could be transported as far away as New York and California. He bought interest in the rail company, the bottling company, and coal mines to fuel his railcars. Everything the company needed to operate he owned and controlled. As a result of this, he could minimize costs and pass on the savings to his customers. *No one* was doing this at the time. Certainly not in the beer world. Before there was Jeff Bezos, there was Adolphus Busch, buying up every vendor he could think of to get his customers their products as fast and as inexpensively as possible.

He was also a sales and marketing genius, a true visionary. Adolphus was a man who believed in brand recognition and awareness long before it was "a thing." He wanted people to think of Budweiser when they thought of beer. He provided bars with promotional light fixtures—proudly displaying the Budweiser name, of course—and even glassware etched with *Budweiser,* as long as they agreed to complete exclusivity in exchange. He made sure to have a controlling interest in bars too. In some cases, he paid bar owners' rents. In return, the bars and taverns could only sell Budweiser beer. Since all customers loved the taste and price, none objected.

He used influencers to spread his brand long before there was TikTok or Instagram, making sure taverns and bars did the work of selling for him. If he could get people to connect personally and viscerally to the product, he knew they'd be customers—friends, that is—for life. That's why he always said, "Making friends is our business." And what do friends do? They tell other friends.

But my great-grandfather could be merciless. Every time he went into a bar that served his beer, he made sure that it was up to his standards. If the beer tasted bad or was served sloppily, there would be hell to pay. He had unbelievably high standards, just like my own father. My father could walk into a seemingly perfect room, and if there were two hundred lights and one was out, he would see it and let everyone know. It would have to be fixed on the spot. Adolphus, like my father, was always pushing the envelope and wanting more out of his company and his people. He always had his sights set on the next big thing. In so many ways, I knew this man. I can hear him, see him, and even smell him—that mixture of beer and cologne, something akin to my father. No, I never met him, but he looms so large in my imagination because I know he lived on in his son, and then in my father.

Adolphus was a man determined to see his company reach the far ends of the earth. He wasn't going to be satisfied just with it hitting every city in America. (My father was like that too.) He was a man who was always thinking generations ahead. He began grooming his first-born son to take over, but Edward died of cancer too early to succeed him, leaving my grandfather, August Sr., to take over the reins. August Sr. would, in turn, train both my father and his oldest son, Adolphus. And my father continued the tradition, starting to groom his firstborn son—August III, my oldest (half) brother—at a young age, pouring all his time and attention into him, because he felt so strongly about keeping the business in the family.

Adolphus and Lilly had thirteen children, nine of which made it to adulthood. He had homes—mansions—in St. Louis, Missouri; Pasadena, California; Cooperstown, New York; and even a villa on the banks of the Rhine in Bad Schwalbach, Germany, which he named after his wife: the Villa Lilly. He opened his home in Pasadena, Ivy Wall, to the public, and it became the first of several Busch Gardens—a beautiful place where the public could gather and bring their families and take in the gorgeous gardens. He counted as his neighbors Andrew Carnegie, J. P. Morgan, and many other influential Americans who were envious of his beautiful home and gardens and who used his mansion as the standard for their own massive homes.

Unlike many of his contemporaries—most notably the infamous and supposed "robber barons" of the Gilded Age, who were ruthless about making money—my great-grandfather believed strongly in making the American dream possible for as many people as were willing to do the work. He worked tirelessly to create jobs so others could afford homes, have a place to work, and live with a sense of pride in their accomplishments. He was a huge philanthropist, gave money to schools like Harvard, and paid and treated his employees well. Money was never his endgame, another part of his legacy. In all the years I grew up with my father, the topic of "making more money" or being "ruthless"—laying off employees, cutting wages, etc.—never was something he discussed. Quite the opposite. For my father, it was always about finding ways to make more jobs, give back to the community, and create parks and areas where families could enjoy themselves—while enjoying Budweiser, of course. Although we were surrounded by wealth, I never got the sense we were better than anyone else. My father, and I am sure his father and his father before that, made sure we all knew the value of a hard day's work and being kind to others—after all, making "friends" (not just money) was the family business.

Ironically enough, making friends paid off in the end. The boy from Germany who arrived in St. Louis with nothing but blind ambition, a dream, and a friendly personality had risen to the highest echelons of society in the American Gilded Age. His dream that his beer would become world renowned had become a reality. And thanks in no small part to him and his brewery in St. Louis, by 1911 the United States surpassed Germany in beer production.

Adolphus had hoped the company would remain in the family forever. He fought mightily in his lifetime to do just that. Though Prohibition was looming, he did his best to lobby and fight hard against it. He took his argument straight to President McKinley and argued that beer was the drink of moderation and temperance. In fact, he believed it had health benefits. He, like my own father, was adamantly against the use of heavy narcotics, straight alcohol, and the state of inebriation. I know my father never believed in drinking until one was drunk. He learned that from his father and grandfather. Adolphus even warned McKinley and many leaders pushing for Prohibition that making it illegal would open up a Pandora's box of crime and dangerous substances that would fill the vacuum left by the moderate beverage he served. (Talk about being a visionary!)

Adolphus didn't live to see Prohibition. He passed away in 1913 after falling ill while hunting with his old friend Carl Conrad, who had helped Adolphus make his dream become a reality. The two were at the Villa Lilly, vacationing in Germany at the time. When he died, his net worth was an estimated $60 million, an astounding figure for that day. His body returned to America aboard his favorite steamer, the *Kronprinz Wilhelm*, and was carried from New York to St. Louis aboard his railcar, the Adolphus, which had been bedecked and styled for a prince. He had designed the railcar himself because he enjoyed arriving everywhere in the utmost style. (It was said that anything considered to be tacky or flashy was called "Buschy" back then!)

My great-grandfather Adolphus was nothing if not extravagant. He spared no expense—even in death. As he was paraded through St. Louis, people stopped working and stepped out in the streets and bowed their heads, as if the King himself had died. And for them, he was the king, the King of Beers, that is. He was so beloved and admired throughout the city that people mourned him as they would family. Tens of thousands of visitors came to his home to pay their respects personally; many of them were factory workers. And it was reported that as many as one hundred thousand people lined the route to the cemetery on the day of his burial.

People had come to love his boisterous and friendly personality. He was a familiar fixture in St. Louis households. He greeted everyone he met with a handshake and even handed out silver coins to children. Wherever he went, children flocked to him. I don't have to imagine the scene. I witnessed his grandson have the same effect on people. I can still see the people swarming around my father in his coach as he snapped the reins and headed out to survey the property. So much of Adolphus lived on in my father. I am sure my father learned a few of Adolphus's tricks when he was a boy, watching the man work the crowds wherever he went. It's impossible not to see how much Adolphus influenced my dad, right down to his flashy clothing, his wavy, coiffed hair, and his booming voice when he yelled. And there was the darker side as well: the side that demanded excellence and perfection and saw anything less as unacceptable. But it worked for them; they got the job done that they set out to do, and people revered and respected them all the same.

When Adolphus died, he had no idea when he handed over the reins to his son August Sr., my grandfather, that it was so close to all being lost, that within a year America would be at war with Germany and the Busch family would have to prove their "American affections." And his worst nightmare would come true seven years after his passing: Prohibition would become law, threatening everything—his legacy, his fortune, his name, his children's birthright, and his company, the Anheuser-Busch Brewing Association.

From the day my grandfather, August Busch Sr., took the reins, he had to fight like hell to save the legacy his father bequeathed to him. And that fight would cost him his life and, in so many ways, would portend the fate of the company just two generations later.

Chapter Two
MY GRANDFATHER, AUGUST ANHEUSER-BUSCH SR.

My grandfather, August Anheuser-Busch, or August Sr. (also known as Papananu by his grandchildren), was born in 1865. He was the third of thirteen children, the second oldest son, and wasn't exactly hoping to ever be the head of his father's company. His eldest brother, Edward, died young, but this didn't guarantee August a place as head of the company. Adolphus wanted everyone to "do their part" and pitch in with the family business, and he used healthy competition as a means to get his sons to perform, creating a bit of rivalry. (My father would tell stories about his own father doing the same, and I witnessed this in my lifetime as well.)

My grandfather's younger brother Adolphus Jr. quickly rose through the ranks and, for all intents and purposes, was being groomed to take over. But the spot was not guaranteed. Adolphus Sr. was pulling for August, wanting his eldest son to be a part of the business. I learned in the book *Gussie,* written by my half sister Lotsie Busch, that Adolphus even sent lengthy letters giving August advice on how to do just that.

My grandfather, however, had other ideas. He didn't have the temperament his father and younger brother had and had little interest in running a brewery. He loved the outdoors and wanted very much to be a cowboy. Adolphus was dismayed, upset that his son wouldn't want to continue the family legacy. So, being the great dad he was, he said, "Okay, you want to be a cowboy? Here's your chaps, hat, pistol, and holster. I'm sending you out West to work on a ranch."

Like many young men of that generation, my grandfather boarded a train and headed off, traveling to New Mexico territory seeking adventure and possibility. August worked as a ranch hand for a whole six months before he came home and told his dad, "I've had enough ranching. I'm ready to go work at the brewery."

Adolphus's bet had paid off. August came back more eager than ever to learn everything he could about helping his brother Adolphus Jr. run the family business. August married Alice Zeismann (who was known to her grandchildren as Gannie) and settled down at Two Busch Place, located on the property of the brewery. They had their first child, Adolphus III, in 1891, followed by daughters Marie and Clara; my father, August Jr.; and their youngest child, Alice. But the life August expected took an unexpected turn.

In 1898, the year before my father was born, Adolphus Jr. died from cancer at just thirty years old. August's brother Peter was considered the black sheep of the family and was not allowed to hold a position at the company due to personal problems. His other brother, Carl, suffered complications at birth and was never able to work at the brewery. So that left August Sr. as the only heir apparent. His fate was sealed.

But city life wasn't for him. Though he'd left his dreams of being a cowboy back at the ranch, he never left his love of country and outdoor life behind. He was a lifelong avid outdoorsman. So, in 1903 August Sr. acquired a large tract of land on the outskirts of St. Louis that had formerly belonged to President Grant, known then as the White Haven property. This, of course, is the land that is now known as Grant's Farm. He hoped it would be his bucolic getaway, where he could partake in all of his outdoor activities—hunting, horseback riding, and raising all sorts of animals.

He wanted to re-create the Bavarian countryside he remembered from his boyhood while hunting with his father. He paid handsomely for elk, sheep, deer, and eventually even an elephant, his beloved Tessie, as well as other exotic animals. Shortly after acquiring the land, the Bauernhof was built. In Germany, many farms possessed a Bauernhof where equipment like horse-drawn carriages were stored and livestock lived. It was also an area where cows and goats were milked as well as butchered for meat and cured. Also inside this structure were living quarters with modern conveniences—heat and plumbing included. This is where the farmhands would meet in the morning to receive their jobs for the day and gather in the evening after work for some beer and food.

My grandfather sought out architects who could build a château reminiscent of Bavarian castles built in the French Renaissance Revival style. It was a costly endeavor, but he took great pains to make it exactly as he envisioned it. Construction started in 1910. But in 1911, on the occasion of their fiftieth wedding anniversary, Lilly and Adolphus decided to give each of their children a mansion to honor the occasion. Adolphus had hoped to give my grandfather, now the heir apparent, One Busch Place, the family mansion. But August asked instead for the money to finance the building of his château on Grant's Farm. At the time, the cost of the home was estimated to be about $300,000.

Once again, my great-grandfather had reservations about his son's decision-making skills. He thought the location was far too remote. It was about twenty miles from the brewery, which in those days meant a half-day's ride over unpaved and hazardous roads. They were especially treacherous when it rained and they turned into mud, or when it was so dry that dust plumes made seeing the road difficult. Needless to say, it was an arduous journey. But most importantly, he argued that a house and grounds of such magnitude would be too expensive to maintain. Adolphus further argued that Grant's Farm would take his focus off running the brewery. But there was no urging or tricking his son this time. August Sr. had made up his mind. He argued that he would need the property to entertain wholesalers, suppliers, retailers, and all the people they did business with, even dignitaries and politicians. As a lover of American history, and President Grant in particular, August insisted that owning the property and keeping it in the Busch family would secure their legacy and commitment to America.

In the end, Adolphus saw the quiet genius of his son and helped finance the project. In some ways, it wasn't a complete risk. August, by then, had proven his business expertise and his preternatural ability to foresee the future and the changing needs of the business. Years earlier, when August Sr. had just returned from working on the ranch and Adolphus was in semiretirement back in Germany, one of the first things he did was come out with a new closing mechanism. At the time, beer bottles were sealed with cork and wire, not unlike champagne. August Sr. was experimenting with the new metal crown cap which William Painter invented back in 1892, but that wasn't yet being widely used. If it worked, it would save time and money. His main objective was to keep the oxygen out because it negatively affected beer. The cap had to fit airtight. Of course, when all was said and done, it worked like a charm.

Back in Germany, Adolphus Sr. was incensed when he heard about his son's bold move to change the bottle without his permission. He was worried August would destroy the business or, worse, ruin the quality and taste of his precious Budweiser. Raging, Adolphus got on the next ship for America. By the time he arrived in St. Louis, he was mad as hell. He went storming into the brewery soon after his arrival. There waiting for him was calm, soft-spoken, logical August Sr. He had prepared a great presentation and showed his father how the new metal crown cap worked. The beer tasted the same and, he argued, it would ultimately save the company loads of money and time. This was the future of bottling. Adolphus was so impressed by his young son's innovation—and his ability to present the information—that he finally felt comfortable that his company and legacy would be left in capable hands. He turned around and boarded the ship back to Germany.

August had it covered.

From what I gather, my grandfather was very different from his own father. He was introverted, loved his solitude in the country, and wasn't as bombastic or gregarious. He might even be called shy or contemplative. He was a deep thinker and a visionary. Adolphus was too, but August Sr. was not as outgoing or social as my great-grandfather.

Nevertheless, he still possessed the charm and charisma that made him magnetic to others. While Adolphus used his charms in an outgoing way, August Sr. was an extremely good listener, gentle, and kind. This equally endeared him to people. Though he had a way with people that made them feel at ease, my grandfather felt much more relaxed with animals, which is something I can relate to myself. He was a brilliant whip; I can attest that it takes enormous skill, precision, intuition, and a sense of calm to command a team of horses pulling a coach. Those skills, I believe, are the same ones he used to lead the brewery through some of its darkest days.

There were other differences between Adolphus and August Sr. that had little to do with temperament and charisma. In some cases, it was environmental. My great-grandfather had the luxury of stepping out of his father's shadow. He came to America alone at an early age and established his own image and brand. In essence, he was given a fresh start. He created the picture he wanted people to see. He lived a life totally on his own terms. He was a masterful brander and knew how to present himself in a way that attracted people to him. Conversely, my grandfather was raised in his father's shadow. He had enormous shoes to fill. Adolphus received no pressure from his own father to maintain an image or take over his company. In fact, Adolphus left his father's company behind to start his own.

August, unfortunately, felt that pressure all his life. He knew all of St. Louis adored his father. From a young age, August felt the responsibility to keep the brewery going and live up to everyone's expectations. I suppose you could say I always felt a connection to my grandfather in this way too. I know what it's like to have giant shoes to fill and to live in the shadow of greatness. Adolphus had done so much for St. Louis, for the country. He was a patriot, beloved by everyone who knew him. I know intimately what it feels like to be compared to my father, and what it was like to live under the scrutinizing eyes of everyone around me. If I pissed off my dad, I would not only hear from my dad, but also from employees and anyone and everyone who had an opinion on the matter. And I wasn't running the company, I was just a kid.

My father, Gussie, and his brother, Adolphus III, started working at the brewery when they became teenagers, learning all the different aspects of the brewing business. Both showed great ability for and interest in the business, but because Adolphus was older, he would get the head position. August Sr., I'm sure, felt that my dad would be a great asset to his brother, and by then the brewery had grown so big that both Adolphus and my dad could coexist, with Adolphus leading the company and Dad as head of day-to-day operations. Still, my grandfather, like his own father, enjoyed creating a sense of rivalry between his sons. He didn't want his boys to get lazy or think that the head position was guaranteed. He liked to keep them on their toes.

August never had it easy. He must have felt an enormous amount of pressure when he took the reins at forty-eight years old in 1913, the year before World War I. He immediately had to fend off anti-German sentiments that plagued the company. He expanded his patriotic efforts and advertising to assure the doubting public that, though his family was from Germany, they were deeply committed patriots. Just as he felt he was able to come up for air and believed he had finally convinced the American public of the Busches' loyalty, Prohibition became law on January 17, 1920.

Imagine the government passing a law that overnight eradicated your entire way of life. It had to feel devastating—like the end of everything. As the story goes, upon hearing the news of the inevitable, my grandfather called his sons, Adolphus III and August Jr., who were both in their twenties, into his office. He knew he was going to need all the help he could get to keep the company afloat for what seemed an uncertain future. Of course, we have the luxury now of knowing that Prohibition would indeed come to a close, but at the time there was no way for my grandfather, father, and uncle to know that. They had to make decisions that would secure the company for the future.

My grandfather was a rational and deliberate man. He felt strongly that he couldn't lose the legacy his father had entrusted to him. I am certain of the tension in the meeting that day—my grandfather's fear and the enormous pressure my father must have felt to help. There was

no doubt an undercurrent of competition, too, between the two brothers. However, August Sr. was shrewd enough to know this wasn't the
time to let egos get in the way; he didn't want to worry about family
rivalry with so much on the line. Picture the scene: the three Busch
family men electrified and illuminating the room as they launched the
best ideas they had in hopes that they would save the company. They
decided the best move was to diversify—get involved in as many industries as possible.

They moved quickly over the next year and leveraged all the business divisions Adolphus had created during his master plan to reduce
costs. They doubled down on their railcar business. They started
making refrigerated trucks. They created an alcohol-free malt beverage, Bevo, to keep the bottles moving. They even made ice cream. Their
real bread and butter, however, became their malt syrup and baker's
yeast divisions. Of course, people didn't just bake with these products. The government may have outlawed the production of alcohol,
but that didn't stop people from brewing their own beer at home. The
birth of home and craft brewing began the day breweries were banned.

Needless to say, it was an enormously stressful time. My grandfather couldn't bring himself to lay anyone off during this time . . . and
he managed to keep all two thousand employees working, despite the
challenges of Prohibition, and later the Depression. This, to me, is
truly an astonishing accomplishment. But it didn't come without sacrifice. As a result, he was forced to borrow millions of dollars, and he
even had to sell all the animals he had spent a fortune on for Grant's
Farm—including his elephant, Tessie.

Just as I loved my elephant (who was also named Tessie), my grandfather adored his. But as the conditions worsened and the money got
tighter, my grandfather knew the right thing to do was sell her. He found
a home for her with Ringling Bros. and Barnum & Bailey Circus. The
day he had to say goodbye to Tessie had to be an especially painful one.
He loved his animals, and it must have been so difficult to watch her go.

But it wasn't the last time they would see each other.

My father told us how one day, a few years after Tessie was sold,

Ringling Bros. came back to St. Louis. Hoping to catch a glimpse of her, my grandfather bought a ticket. Before the show, the circus would parade its animals down the street to the circus tent. As soon as he saw Tessie marching in the line of elephants, he called out: "Tessie!" Tessie, like all elephants, was incredibly intelligent. They never forget, especially those they love; I can attest to every bit of that. When she heard my grandfather's voice, she broke free from the line, trumpeted with joy, and walked right up to where he was standing. The two shared a moment in front of the crowd. Witnesses said they saw my grandfather shaken and in tears.

He had lost his beloved friend, and he was losing his company. Even after Prohibition ended and things returned to normal, he was never able to buy Tessie back. He tried, but the circus wouldn't allow it because Tessie had become the matriarch of the circus's elephant herd. But the loss of Tessie wasn't the worst of it. He was exhausted from the constant work and the pressure to keep his employees paid, and he struggled with health ailments, a result of years of stress.

On many occasions during the darkest days of Prohibition and the Depression, my father tried to lift his father's spirits. One story he often told us as kids is that he rode his horse, Spot, up the steps of the Big House, down the massive hallway, and into his father's bedroom, just to make his sad and sick father laugh.

Spot was a legendary horse. We often heard stories about how my dad was the only one who could ride him without being bucked off. Dad bought Spot from a cowboy who hated to sell him but needed the money. He paid the cowboy a large sum and was bucked off for eleven days straight but was determined to ride him, and he finally did. He went on to win a lot of money on bets with people who thought they could ride Spot without being bucked off! It must have brought my grandfather great joy to see his son riding Spot. I can't help but wonder if my grandfather understood the symbolic gesture, even if my father wasn't aware of it at the time: if my father could ride a horse like Spot and not be bucked off, his father could fight his illness and make it through another day.

Indeed, August never stopped fighting during Prohibition. He met with congressional committees and two presidents—Warren G. Harding and Calvin Coolidge. He was tireless in his efforts to overturn what he felt was an unfair and hypocritical law. Those who could afford alcohol were still getting it, and everyone knew it. He even wrote his now-famous *Open Letter to the American People*, in which he once again presented his case logically and soundly, as he so often did with his father when trying to get his way. He sent the pamphlet to every senator, congressman, and even the then-governor of New York, Franklin D. Roosevelt. In the pamphlet, my grandfather argued that Americans returning to work was more important than Prohibition. America was in a deep Depression and Prohibition wasn't helping matters. Reopening breweries wouldn't just help the breweries, bottlers, distributors, and bar owners, it would also help farmers, coal miners, and even railroad workers, not to mention the countless other industries that relied on all of the above. Prohibition was harming America, not helping it. Crime had increased, and people hadn't stopped drinking—in fact they were turning to more dangerous ways of entertaining themselves.

Franklin Roosevelt heeded August's words, and his presidential campaign included the promise to repeal the Eighteenth Amendment. When all was said and done, Roosevelt won the election. As he promised, just nine days after his inauguration, on March 13, 1933, he asked Congress to immediately authorize the sale of beer. He referenced beer only, as it was 3.2 percent alcohol. Both the House and Senate agreed, and April 8 was set as the day on which the sale of beer could resume.

My grandfather had been rejoicing and preparing for April 8 since the election. He had to get the plant ready for the production and bottling of beer again, not to mention source all the ingredients as well as prepare for its distribution. They needed to get a lot of bottles to a very demanding public. It was about this time that the company went public; before that, all the stock was held by the family.

One of the benefits of surviving Prohibition was that Anheuser-Busch lost most of its competition. Almost 90 percent of brewers disappeared over the thirteen years that Prohibition and the Depression had ravaged the country. Nevertheless, my grandfather didn't take this position for granted. Not ones to rest on their laurels, my grandfather, dad, and uncle decided that now was the time to establish Budweiser as the King of Beers. If beer was back, they wanted to be leading the pack. They knew they could achieve this through advertising and creating a brand synonymous with beer.

My father, who by then was general manager of brewing operations, had an inspiring idea. He asked August Sr. for money for advertising. His father agreed but had no idea what his son was up to. Secretly, my father used that money to purchase sixteen Clydesdales. Why? They are the king of horses. My father had recalled that when his grandfather Adolphus was in charge, he would conduct weekly inspections of his teams from a viewing stand. As a young boy, my father remembered seeing his own father and grandfather standing side by side as they watched the teams of horses and wagons carrying the crates of beer out of the brewery. Each driver would make sure their wagon and horses were impeccable. My great-grandfather and grandfather would award the best-looking team with a twenty-five dollar reward.

My father envisioned harnessing the iconic history of the company to showcase Budweiser as America's beer. He thought that if he and his brother, Adolphus, could restore the old wagons, load them with crates of Budweiser, and use a team of Clydesdales to pull them into both New York City and Washington, DC, on April 8, it would create a sensation and secure Budweiser and Anheuser-Busch's future as the King of Beers. But mostly, knowing my father the way I do, I think he wanted to surprise and impress his own father.

Without August knowing, my father rounded up sixteen Clydesdales and covertly used the circular stable in the brewery to restore the old wagons to their once-majestic glory. My father even tracked down the best driver from the old wagon-hauling days, Billy Wales, who had left St. Louis for Chicago. I can just see my father, a young man, filled with excitement and hope, working to bring a smile to his hardworking father. Even though the dark days of Prohibition were now behind them, my grandfather was still suffering physically. And my father, who always loved to make people smile and be happy, pulled out all the stops with this particular surprise.

When the team was secured, the wagon polished to perfection, the beer loaded and ready to go, and Billy at the whip, my father ran over to August Sr.'s office. He told August he had a new automobile to show him. When they walked across the street to the stable, my father rushed ahead and swung open the doors. He then watched as his father broke down in tears of shock, joy, and amazement, rendered speechless at the sight of Billy, the gleaming wagons, and the perfectly coiffed horses bedecked with ribbons in their manes and tails, white feathers or stockings, and shiny golden-brown hair similar to a crisp pilsner. I am sure my father was overcome, too, at the sight of his own father being so overjoyed.

On the plant floor, August Sr., my father, and my uncle posed next to a crate of beer destined for Washington, DC, a special delivery for the man himself, Franklin D. Roosevelt, who had finally put an end to Prohibition. That crate was sent via plane, then by truck, and then boarded onto a wagon pulled by a team of six Clydesdales. At the same time, another crate was shipped and traveled its final leg of the journey in a wagon pulled by a second team of horses to New York City for a flashy arrival of its own. Crowds gathered in the New York streets as the Clydesdales made their way down Fifth Avenue to the Empire State Building, where ardent anti-Prohibition front man, Al Smith, was waiting to give his live radio address to the country. Back in Washington, DC, as other crates of beer arrived for Roosevelt (clearly, everyone had the same idea), only one beer arrived with an entrance worthy of a king—aboard a wagon, hitched to a team of beautiful horses. With every resounding *clop, clop, clop* of the Clydesdales, everyone in Washington, New York, and America saw and heard what my father had so concisely announced on radio waves the night before: "Beer is back."

The relief and joy were short-lived, though—at least for my father, his brother, and my grandfather. The Depression, Prohibition, and the stress of bringing the company back to brewing took a brutal toll on the nervous system and health of August Sr. My grandfather was said to suffer from gout, a terrible disease caused by an increase in uric acid in the bloodstream that can be exacerbated by stress. It's a complex form of arthritis, an inflammatory disease that causes the joints and feet to swell, sometimes making it impossible to even stand. It's incredibly painful. Ironically, one of the major sources of uric acid is alcohol. And like his father before him, who suffered dropsy—an inability to remove fluids from the body—my grandfather suffered from similar distress. He had heart disease and edema and, as a result, spent many days in indescribable pain. As we all know now, pain does things to your brain. And people can talk very freely now about the harmful effects of stress on the body. But my grandfather didn't have those tools at his disposal. I am sure he was depressed and had been desiring some form of relief for some time. In fact, I am sure of it. Because that is the only explanation for what happened next.

Less than one year after Prohibition ended, in February 1934, my grandfather asked his butler for his pearl-handled .32-caliber pistol—a pistol I know so well because it sat in my father's bedside table throughout my childhood. When his butler turned around, my grandfather shot himself in the chest. Unfortunately, the bullet missed his heart. Once again, my grandfather suffered needlessly for several minutes as his wife watched him die. My father was in New York but, as soon as he heard the news, rushed to his mother's side.

The only note my grandfather left said, "Goodbye precious Momie and adorable children." He so loved his wife and children, but the pain he experienced was beyond anything most people could bear in one lifetime. There are pills now that people can take for fluid retention, pain, and heart disease. I'd like to think that if he got the help he needed, he would have stuck around to see his company thrive.

My grandfather gave his life for the business he loved. He cared deeply about continuing a legacy started by his father and wanted to leave it for his own kids. My father was almost thirty-five years old when his father took his own life at sixty-eight. August must have known that he had earned enough money to live a comfortable life with his family, but he also knew that his employees depended on their jobs at the brewery to feed their families. He was driven to succeed for them, for his family, for his father's legacy—no matter what the cost, even his own health. It's hard to imagine how much he suffered, not to mention his wife and kids and all who loved him and now had to live without him.

One of the saddest parts of his life, I think, is that he never got to see the fruits of his labor and sacrifice, like his father did. He died before he could see the brewery return to its glory. And then there was the pain it caused his wife, Alice, our Gannie, whom he cared for so deeply and whom he was so faithful and true to throughout his whole marriage. He adored her.

When I think of my father losing his father in such a tragic way, I feel so much compassion for him and understand him so much better, especially how he was as both a man and a father. One thing I will always remember my father telling us children was that he only walked on his father's left side, and he wouldn't think of passing him on a horse or on foot. He did so out of respect. As a child, I recall doing the same with my father. We children always walked beside him and never in front of him. We adored our father and looked at him as if he were a god, and I understand that is exactly how my father felt about August Sr. His loss must have been unimaginable.

———

My grandfather was a boy who wanted to be a cowboy, ride horses, and spend his days in the country with his wife and children, but he fulfilled his father's wishes and managed to keep the brewery going despite impossible obstacles. In the end, he died a tragic death.

Unlike his own father, who was buried in a flashy mausoleum, August Sr. wanted no fanfare in his death. Unassuming to the end—the good soldier, as it were—he lived his life out of duty to his father, brewery, wife, children, and country and wanted little else than a tombstone engraved with *August A. Busch*. He asked to be buried under the trees on a hillside that overlooked his home in what is now the family plot. Because, in the end, that was what truly mattered to him. No, not just the "château"—or what we called the "Big House"—but Grant's Farm and all that it represented: a place he loved, where animals and nature thrived, where his beloved wife and children were, and where he could, at least for a few hours a day, be the cowboy he had always dreamed of being.

He was a Busch through and through and embodied everything that meant—duty, loyalty, love of family, hard work, and being a friend to everyone. And he left behind two heartbroken sons, vying for control of their father's hard-won legacy.

Chapter Three
DARLING GUSSIE

The Greenbrier
White Sulphur Springs
West Virginia
March 16, 1920

My Darling Gussie,

    I heard from Adolphus today that you have entered upon your new career with great enthusiasm, and I wish to assure you that I am pleased beyond words, fully realizing that you will gain an immense amount of knowledge, which will be so useful and important in making you one of the leading bankers of this country.

    Have requested Mr. Gengenbach to supply you with an abundance of literature on finance and the banking business in general. I hope you and Gengenbach are still striving to become members of the Noonday Club; this is most essential, as it will put you in close touch with men of affairs.

    I trust my dear good boy will avail himself of every advantage and fulfill the position of every employee for several months, so that your foundation is built upon practical and sound knowledge.

    You are now entering your twenty-first anniversary (manhood)

to it shall be the strife of my life to make you the youngest president
of the largest institutions in St. Louis, when you obtain the age of
twenty-seven or -eight. All I ask, dear Gussie, in return is for you
never to gamble, always be the most exacting in every statement
that you make, be an example of sincerity and integrity so that you
will be beloved to all.

> *From one who loves his children*
> *the best on earth,*
> *Your Daddy*

Sorting through my father's boxes not long ago, I found this wonderful letter. My grandfather, August Sr., was writing to my father on the occasion of his twenty-first birthday (which was on March 28, 1920) from The Greenbrier hotel in West Virginia, where he went for rest and relaxation as a remedy for his many ailments.

My father, then a young man, had joined the Lafayette South Side Bank in St. Louis, where he started as a traveling bonds salesman. My great-grandfather Adolphus founded the South Side Bank in 1891. It was one of the many ways he diversified the company from the outset. Though from the outside it may seem odd for a Busch to not be working in the brewery, it was, in fact, part of the greater plan, especially if the worst should happen during Prohibition and the entire beer business went bust. But, if that didn't happen, he would still need to understand the world of business and finance. Nevertheless, I believe it was always my father's intention to work at the brewery, so banking was a crucial part of that. I am also certain that, since his brother, Adolphus, was the oldest, he knew he wasn't going to be the first in line to take over the brewery. My father wasn't particularly interested in playing second fiddle—ever. He would bide his time, learn as much as he could, and be ready to take over when the time was right.

It was well known that Adolphus III shared the same temperament as his father, August Sr., and was a somewhat calm, laid-back, and introverted individual. My father, on the other hand, was anything but.

He was loud, had a booming voice, and didn't mince words. In 1927 his mother wrote him letters urging him to stop using "curse words" and "subdue" his voice, reminding him of his "noble fine character." She stated, "Your language is unworthy of you." She further said that my father would "be admired by everyone if you follow my advice." When she was saying *everyone*, she most definitely meant her husband, August Sr., who was not someone who admired loud or swearing young men. And who, in his own letters, beseeched my father "never to gamble, always be the most exacting in every statement that you make, be an example of sincerity and integrity so that you will be beloved to all." In every letter, it became clear to me that my grandmother favored my father and wanted him to succeed. She even often went so far as to call him "the apple of my life." She was pulling for my dad to one day become the head of the company, even in the early years when he wasn't at the brewery.

Though, at the time, my father had no formal education in finance, my grandfather was betting on his capable son. August Sr. had hoped that Gussie would learn banking just as he had learned the brewing business, by working every job and in every aspect of the business. This, of course, sounds extremely familiar to me because my father expected each of us to learn the business—anything we did, really—from the ground up, whether it was mucking stalls, cleaning out the pigpen, baling hay, or working the concessions on Grant's Farm. No job was too menial. Nothing was beneath a Busch family member. Walking in another's shoes was part of "making friends." Knowing what others were going through or were up against was key too. You learned this way before you became the manager or the head of the department or the leader of the company. You had to be hands-on and know the job inside out. I am sure August Sr. learned that from Adolphus and passed it on to his son, and my dad passed it on to each of us. It's a rare thing to see—in writing—the family "way" of doing business. I had always understood that this was something my father had absorbed or learned from his father, but to see it written down in my grandfather's hand is something truly remarkable to behold.

My father dropped out of school in the sixth grade. The family legend is that he climbed out of the schoolhouse window onto a tree and ran to a whorehouse and never looked back. Whether this is true or not, we know he received the remainder of his education from the "University of the Brewery"—trying out every position there as well. I can only surmise that he chose banking because his father was concerned about the brewery's viability. At the time, there was so much uncertainty in the beer business, and my grandfather knew he had to have other options. From what I gathered, he was placing his hopes that his "darling" Gussie would become one of the youngest presidents of the largest banks in the country and help secure the Busch name and legacy should the brewery fold during Prohibition.

Though my father was working at the bank and traveling far and wide, selling bonds all over the United States, he was still very much involved in the brewery. In a 1922 letter he wrote to his first wife, Marie Church, he said that the "business" was losing money and was in bad shape. They were hoping to make money on the "glue"—which was what they called corn because in the brewing process corn becomes very sticky—but it wasn't doing as well as expected. The brewery's survival was a cause of great consternation for him, his father, and his brother.

In those letters to his young wife, he expressed how tired he was and how difficult it was to sell bonds while worrying about keeping the brewery open—and to be away from her. Marie, a beautiful young debutante who fell for my father's "riding" abilities, was afflicted with bronchitis and lung issues and couldn't tolerate the St. Louis heat and humidity. She spent many months away—mainly in California, where it was drier and cooler. She wrote at length about the difficult conditions aboard the train—the dust and heat—as she made her way back and forth.

The two were basically children when they wedded in a lavish society affair on April 17, 1918. My father had just turned nineteen years old. Over the next three years, he faced Prohibition, started a new career, and set out to start a family of his own. In 1923, they welcomed my oldest half sister, Lilly Marie Christy Busch, on December 19. Everyone was hoping for a boy, but my grandmother, Gannie, wrote to her son and was encouraging, saying, "All we care is that the baby is healthy," and "We know she will be beautiful if it's a girl." Four years later, on July 19, 1927, my half sister Carlota "Lotsie" Clark Chouteau Busch was born, named in part after her mother's side of the family, which descended from William Clark, who led the Lewis and Clark Expedition for Thomas Jefferson.

They lived the life of high society in a twenty-three-room mansion, a gift from my grandfather, which was one of the most prominent estates in St. Louis at the time. It was illuminated with giant floodlights from the east and west sides and was highly visible as the center of the social scene. However, despite their deep love for each other, Gussie and Marie spent most of their young marriage apart. My father split his time between brewery work and the bank and spent a lot of time at Grant's Farm, while Marie often sought treatment and relief for her ailments in Santa Barbara.

They wrote letters back and forth, sharing their daily misadventures. In one letter Gussie explained to Marie how one night his two dogs—the actual siblings of the famed silent-movie star from the '20s, Rin Tin Tin—woke him up and proceeded to lose their minds, viciously attacking him. My father attributed it to the full moon because they had never done anything like that before. He counted on them as a means of security, keeping him safe from prowlers or trespassers, but he had never been on the other end of their attacks. He scrambled to get away and had to roll up a sheet and cover his arm in an attempt to block them and escape the bedroom unharmed. But they attacked his arm so ferociously that he suffered from serious pain in his arms for years to come.

Through the letters, I can see my father clearly missed her a great deal, but that was only half the story. What the letters don't reveal is just how much he enjoyed the life of a bachelor and carousing with his friends. The 1920s, for the most part, were my father's formative years, what would've translated for most kids as their "college days." But unlike college kids, my father didn't go to school; instead, he had a sickly wife, two daughters, and the added pressure of becoming the youngest president of one of the largest institutions in St. Louis by the age of twenty-seven, all while helping his family keep the brewery afloat during Prohibition. He frequented speakeasies and parties—it was the Roaring Twenties and the Jazz Age. Being the handsome, wealthy, and charming guy he was, he had no problem attracting all kinds of young beautiful women to vie for his attention. He took up boxing and started what he dubbed the Knights of the Cauliflower Ear: a group of men who loved to box and raise hell together. He had run-ins with gangsters and bootleggers. I remember him telling me about the time he met Al Capone, ostensibly over some union business. He went into the meeting not knowing exactly what to expect but also knowing Capone might kill him. The two hit it off well. In other words, my father walked away from the exchange without a bullet in his head.

Gregarious, outgoing, and the life of every party, my father was everyone's "Darling Gussie"—his mother's, his father's, his wife's, and even a cadre of lovers and friends. Almost everyone who wrote Gussie addressed him first with "Darling." Though, on occasion, Marie took to calling him "my bad boy" and "my one and only love." Though not exactly true, my father called her "my only love" and signed his letters, "the one who loves you best, Gussie."

Within a decade, however, their relationship seemed to be souring, at least from my father's perspective. He had always had a roving eye and a reputation as a ladies' man, but we know now that he was in fact cheating on Marie. He had begun a serious relationship with a woman, and apparently, Marie was devastated. Though the letters don't indicate who she was (there are several possibilities), it may very well have been my father's second wife, Elizabeth Dozier. Though Marie's obituary says she died of pneumonia after fighting the flu, which my father had also had two weeks before her death, many people in the family believe that Marie, just thirty years old, died of a broken heart. She was so sensitive and must have given up the will to live, knowing my father most likely would leave her for this other woman if she were to survive her bout with pneumonia.

Though my father and Marie were most likely on their way to divorce, he was still shaken by her loss and overcome with grief. I don't think it's unfathomable to presume he may have even been tinged with guilt, or at the very least, regret. Even though their marriage was not a happy one by the end, he was still a devoted father and felt the enormous responsibility of taking care of his young girls, just six and three at the time. And Marie had been beloved by everyone—especially my grandmother, Gannie. Her loss was a blow to the entire family. My grandmother wrote my father the morning after hearing the news of Marie's death:

Darling . . . God has taken from you my beloved daughter, whom I loved more than anything in this world. She was always a comfort and a joy . . . There never was a more beautiful and more unselfish character. She loved you and her two darling babies devotedly and was so fond of you. God bless you and comfort you. Gussie dear! My heart aches with grief for you and my darling little parental grandbabies. Write me a few words when you have time, with love and devotion.

Momie

While I am sure my father was devastated by the loss, in short order he took his relationship public with the socialite Elizabeth Overton Dozier, who was married to Lewis Dozier, president of the St. Louis Country Club at the time. When August Sr. tried to join the St. Louis Country Club many years earlier, the Busch family was apparently not "blue blood" enough for them because they were beer drinkers and not wine connoisseurs. As was customary back in the late nineteenth and early twentieth centuries, one had to "descend" from a certain lineage (old money) to be accepted into society. My grandfather wanted no part of that nonsense, so he started Sunset Country Club instead, one of the first in the area that also offered a swimming pool and served beer, of course.

Perhaps being shut out of the country club was part of the attraction of it all for my father. He loved nothing better than a challenge. Gussie and Elizabeth had been carrying on an affair in secret until, according to the family legend, one night my father rode up to the forbidden country club on horseback. He went in, took Elizabeth by the hand, and hoisted her up onto his horse. Together they rode off into the moonlight, leaving behind her husband, the country club, and the snobbish members who had rejected his father and family.

If it hadn't already been written down somewhere, after that night, no Busch was allowed into the St. Louis Country Club. Although that changed about forty years later in the 1970s when my father was allowed to join. In short order, he called up his friends, a bunch of big drinkers who liked to party, smoke, and get crazy—nicknamed the Wrecking Crew—and they went into the club and did $10,000 worth of damage.

Elizabeth divorced Dozier in September of 1933 and, in less than a month, married my father. She had three children with her first husband and was awarded custody. So the three children joined Lilly and Lotsie in the mansion he had shared with Marie. At that time, the ever-supportive Gannie wrote another letter to my father, approving of Elizabeth as well and wishing him the best of luck.

It must have been a busy and tumultuous year. A few years prior, South Side Bank had successfully merged with Farmers and Merchants Trust and had closed temporarily for restructuring. My father was now back full-time at the brewery. He had been elected to the board of directors, was serving as the vice president and general manager, and was helping Adolphus run the company. For a brief time, my father was enjoying newfound love and a bit of success at the brewery—thanks to the initial bounce from the end of Prohibition—and he hoped that his father's health would soon return.

But in less than a year, my grandfather would be dead, Adolphus would become the president of Anheuser-Busch, and my father would suddenly find himself the head of a growing brood of children. Within two years of their marriage, my father and Elizabeth welcomed Elizabeth Overton Busch (Junior). Two years later, in 1937, my father would finally welcome a male heir—August Busch III.

For the next several years, my father raised his new family and helped his brother, Adolphus, run the family company. But then on December 7, 1941, the unthinkable happened. The United States was attacked. By the beginning of 1942, most able-bodied men in the United States enlisted to join the fight. My father was one of them. Though he never served overseas, he worked his way up through the ranks from major to colonel and spent a lot of time in Washington, DC. On December 28, 1942, my grandmother wrote him on the occasion of his becoming Major August Busch, United States Army:

> *Gussie darling,*
>
> *In spirit, I will be with you on the thirty-first. I hope and pray the good Lord will grant us a victory in '43 and that we will be reunited in peace once more. My heart is filled with good wishes for you and yours!*
>
> *With endless love and a big hug and kiss,*
> *Always Devotedly, Mother*

Contrary to Gannie's hopes, the war would drag on for another three years. Gussie helped to establish precedents and procedures for organizing the nation's industries to work as a singular unit—the United States' industries were a huge help in the war effort. Anheuser-Busch helped build fuselages and engines that were used for tanks. They also coordinated the making of yeast pills for the soldiers, which helped them stay strong.

One of my father's last acts before heading off to war was to approve the company's marketing plan which was to support the US's participation in the war effort. The plan was to make sure that all Budweiser campaigns devoted 95 percent of their messages to supporting the US government's war efforts. One of the many World War II–era ads featured the "A & Eagle" among warplane gliders. The ad was to show that the planes were made with parts from Budweiser's Refrigeration Division. Below the copy describing the planes, it says, "In addition to supplying the armed forces with glider parts, gun turret parts and foodstuffs, Anheuser-Busch produces materials which go into the manufacture of: Rubber, Aluminum, Munitions, Medicines, B Complex Vitamins, Hospital Diets, Baby Foods, Bread and other Bakery products, Vitamin-fortified cattle feeds, Batteries, Paper, Soap and textiles—to name a few." As per the agreement to reserve 5 percent of the copy for advertising actual Budweiser beer, in small italics in the left-hand corner of the ad, it reads, "Incidentally, our Refrigeration Division was created many years ago as a result of experience gained in making millions of tons of ice to produce the world's most popular beer." It's not an overstatement that Budweiser's contributions were essential to the winning of World War II. And my father was indeed the mastermind behind it.

With his ad campaigns during World War II, my father elevated branding and advertisements not just for beer but for all products. He showed that Budweiser was more than a product, it was something you could aspire to become. Drinking Budweiser made you a patriot, a true American, someone who was helping the boys at home and abroad. He made the "experience" of buying and drinking beer a part of something "bigger than oneself." Budweiser instantly became more than a product, it became a message: Budweiser is America.

The message stuck. I still can't think of a more American brand than Budweiser. Coke, maybe, but there was no product then, or one now, that so exemplified what it meant to be an American. What my father had done with the Clydesdales—harkening back to America's founding—seemed like small potatoes in comparison to his World War II campaign. He took the company and the beer to new heights. I think my father instinctively knew the power storytelling had to close a deal and make a sale. He knew that if he could tell people a great story, convince them of their value, assure their friendship and loyalty and how much they mattered, he could sell them anything. He wasn't wrong. And soon the competition—all brands, really—followed on his Clydesdales and coach's well-trodden path.

In 1945, with the war over, my father returned to St. Louis to work at the brewery full-time under his brother's leadership. In 1946 he was finally honorably discharged as a colonel and awarded the Legion of Merit for his pioneering efforts and ensuring a new type of coordination between industry and the army ordinance. That same year, on August 29, 1946, the family was hit by another horrible twist of fate. After being hospitalized for several days due to a stomach cancer diagnosis, Adolphus died. It came as quite a shock to everyone. He had been ill, but no one expected him to die so suddenly. Not long before the cancer diagnosis, Adolphus had a physical and his doctors gave him a clean bill of health. But when he discovered a lump and went back to the doctor, he was immediately diagnosed. The cause of death is listed as cardiac complications or cerebral hemorrhage. Regardless, it was sudden and happened so fast no one could even process it. My father put it this way: "He was here today and gone tomorrow."

The brewery and my father were devastated. Making matters worse, prior to Adolphus's death, my dad and he had a major falling out. Apparently, my father had ordered a million dollars' worth of beer to be dumped because it wasn't up to his exacting standards, and it was past the expiration date. Adolphus believed that while it was not "perfect," the beer was acceptable for shipment, but my father wouldn't hear of it. He was in charge of quality control and ordered to proceed with the dumping. Adolphus was extremely angry with my father for disregarding his orders. In response, my father threatened resignation, and the board had to talk him out of it. My father was the most competitive person I ever met, and the notion of playing second fiddle to his brother, especially after enjoying so much freedom and authority during the war, must have been a hard pint to swallow. Up until the moments of Adolphus's death, my father very much considered leaving the brewery and finding something else to do.

Then, overnight, my father became the president of Anheuser-Busch. My own brother, another Adolphus, has said, knowing our father the way we do, that it was probably the happiest day of his life. That sounds harsh, but our father was nothing if not ambitious. In all likelihood, though, he was both—at once elated to run the brewery but devastated by the personal loss. A letter from one of his paramours at the time, Ida, reveals the pain my father was experiencing:

> *Darling, I never knew how much and how thoroughly a human being is able to love. I realized it now because your pain is so completely mine and my heart aches as if it were yours, my sweet. I wish it would be a small consolation for you to know that everything of me belongs to you and maybe God has led me in your life so that my deep love for you might help to carry on and heal the wound that the death of your beloved brother has inflicted upon you.*

Another lover at the time (and yes, he was still married to Elizabeth) wrote similarly:

> *My darling, I would have given anything in this world to have been able to call you tonight, but I knew that I hadn't the right. I mustn't even send this note to your home for fear of someone opening your mail. It was such a terrible, terrible shock, even after you have told me how dreadfully ill he [Adolphus] was. Yes, I guess we should thank God now that he didn't suffer very long. Death is so tragic to those who are left behind, but so often it is such a blessed release for the one who goes. And even though we miss them so terribly, if we really love them, I think we are grateful that they are where there is no more suffering and pain, don't you? I know what a loss it is for you, my darling, and it hurts me, to know you will. I know you also will have to be extremely brave about it for your mother. For your mother's sake, you will be her only son, and she will need you more than ever. I realize that it will probably be a very long time before I will see you again, my darling, but always know that you have my heart and my thoughts are with you every minute of every hour. I love you, darling.*

————

Now fully immersed in the company business—which as we know was making friends—my father was constantly traveling and entertaining, which no doubt took a toll on his marriage to Elizabeth. It was clear from letters between the two that their relationship was on the rocks and that they were living separate lives by 1948. Things had deteriorated so much that my father moved in with his daughter, Lotsie, in an apartment in the Bauernhof on Grant's Farm. She, too, was going through a divorce. She was a dear companion and sounding board for my father, incredibly intelligent, and in many ways a source of good counsel and sage advice. She had remarkable business instincts, and had she been a man, she could have run the company, but times being what they were back then, that wasn't an option.

In 1948 my father flew to Europe to inspect hops fields, in addition to picking out some world-famous schnauzers. In his travels, he found himself dining at the finest restaurant in Lucerne, the Old Swiss House. He was greeted at the door by the hostess, also the daughter of the owner. She was one of the most beautiful and stately women he had ever laid eyes on. It was love at first sight—at least for my father.

The hostess was just twenty-one years old (the same age as his daughter, Lotsie) and seemed unfazed by him. She simply walked my father to his table. My father started flirting, almost immediately. The girl's parents were clearly uncomfortable with my father's overtures, but he just couldn't get over her beauty and charming personality. Before the night was over, he asked her if he could meet with her the next day and if she would help him find a schnauzer. They spent the next day together traveling around, ostensibly looking for schnauzers but really getting to know each other. One day led to another. My father couldn't bring himself to leave, so he decided to spend a few extra days in Switzerland courting her.

It wasn't too long after that first meeting that he invited her to America. Her father was totally against it. He had spent years during World War II trying desperately to hide his daughter from military men, fending off the Germans, Russians, and Americans who traveled to Switzerland on their leaves for relaxation and healing—and, of course, to have a little fun with beautiful Swiss women. Now that the war was over and he thought the coast was clear, in comes my father: twenty-eight years older than her, with confidence, good looks, and unbeknownst to him, a multimillion-dollar corporation in America. He objected outright, but his daughter Gertrude—my mother—knew exactly what she wanted. She told her father she was going to America with the handsome, smooth-talking—and married—charmer.

My father headed back to the United States, and she soon followed. They stayed at the shooting lodge. My father introduced Gertrude, who went by Trudy, to Lotsie, and the two hit it off instantly. In her book *Gussie,* Lotsie noted that Trudy had a "piquant," or sharp, sense of humor and that she loved spending time with her. My father showed Trudy all over Grant's Farm, taking her on coaching rides and even down to the brewery. He wanted her to see his life in its entirety because he very much wanted her to be involved in every aspect of it. He made his proposal: "I need someone at my side." And by that he meant he needed someone to help run the company and entertain. I'll never forget my mom telling me the story of how he pleaded with her. "He asked, 'Can you just give me twenty great years?'"

Shortly after, against her parents' wishes, Trudy left her life in Switzerland behind and moved in with my father. For several years, they shared the apartment with Lotsie. My father's marriage met its bitter end in 1952. As a part of the settlement, Elizabeth would remain in the house on Lindell with Elizabeth and August (teenagers at the time), and my father was finally free to marry Trudy. Once again, my father moved on from his "old family" to start a new one. Though I wasn't born then or aware of how painful this could be (my time would come soon enough), I understand now how supposed "business" decisions between father and son could become extremely personal.

On March 27, 1952, my father—fifty-three years old, the president of Anheuser-Busch, and everyone's (but his ex-wife's) "darling,"—was married to the young, beautiful, multilingual, and outdoorsy Gertrude "Trudy" Buholzer, with the "piquant" sense of humor and endless charm, in Hot Springs, Arkansas, at the Majestic Hotel by a justice of the peace. Her parents were not in attendance. But the couple didn't need anyone's approval; they were doing things their way now and were about to transform Grant's Farm, the brewery, St. Louis, and the Busch family— forever.

Part Two

CAMELOT

Chapter Four
SPRINGTIME FOR THE HAPPIEST FAMILY IN THE WORLD

Don't let it be forgot,
that once there was a spot,
for one brief shining moment
that was known as Camelot.

—Camelot, the musical

I recall the Midwest best as I think upon the demarcation of the seasons. I think of *my life*, like most people, in terms of seasons. My childhood, along with my young mother's marriage to my father, was springtime—punctuated by burgeoning nature, births of animals and children, flowers, laughter, joy, visits from strangers and dignitaries, and so many new beginnings. It was a time of seemingly endless youth and happiness.

My father, already in the autumn of his life by the time he married my mother, was trying desperately to hold on to his own proverbial spring and summer. He did so by holding fast to my young mother and his new growing brood of children—seven by the time all was said and done. Between their wedding in 1952 and 1966, the year of the birth of my youngest sister, Christina—my father's "Honey Bee," the apple of his eye, and the cutest baby I ever laid eyes on—my father had not only created a fairy-tale "royal" family, but a very real, thriving empire. During those prodigious fourteen years, my father expanded everything in his kingdom: his family, his brewery, his properties, his amusement parks, a baseball franchise, and his legacy. All this growth was no doubt due in large part to the roles my mother and we children played in the creation of the fairy-tale life that he was selling. And for a time, it didn't feel like a business or a fairy tale. It felt real. We all believed it was and that there would be no "The End." We all lived as if this brief and shining moment would last forever.

That is not to say that my father's previous wives, Marie and Elizabeth, didn't play a huge part. Marie brought glamour and beauty into my father's life and whatever his failings as a husband, he loved her deeply, and her death was hard on him. She exposed him to the world of Hollywood and made introductions to the Hollywood elite, like Douglas Fairbanks, while she stayed in the Miramar Hotel in Santa Barbara and many glamorous Los Angeles hotels during the hot St. Louis summers. Many of these relationships would last decades. He even knew and became friends with Walt Disney, who many say was inspired by my great-grandfather's Ivy Wall, the forerunner of Busch Gardens, Pasadena. He was especially drawn to the gardens and the family attractions. Marie was a beautiful socialite who opened doors for my dad and helped him make connections in California that endured.

Likewise, Elizabeth supported my father in his business pursuits and stood by him through some of the most difficult years—pulling the company out of the Depression, weathering World War II, and finally supporting him through the death of his brother and becoming president of Anheuser-Busch. In both marriages, my father benefited enormously from these women and their support and love. I truly believe that he loved them and that he was happy in the beginning of their relationships, just as he was happy with my mother in the beginning of theirs.

When my parents were first married, they remained in the small apartment they had shared with Lotsie. It's safe to say those were very happy years for the two. They were content just to be together.

Shortly after their wedding, my mom got pregnant and had a miscar-
riage. But in 1953 she gave birth to my brother Adolphus, followed
by Beatrice, Peter, and Trudy in quick succession. Needless to say, by
1957, it was getting a bit crowded in the Bauernhof apartment. At
some point, Gannie wrote a note to my father from her smaller house,
also known as "the cottage," which she had built on the Grant's Farm
property after my grandfather died. She told my dad, in no uncertain
terms, that it was time to move. The Big House had remained empty
since my grandfather's passing. Though it had been open for a time as
a museum, visitors began stealing items and it was quickly shut down
again. My grandmother felt it was a waste for such a beautiful place to
sit empty, though she couldn't bring herself to live in the place without her beloved husband. She decided the next best thing was to have
my father, now president of her husband's company, move into the
Big House so that he and my mother could raise their children there,
run the farm, and use it as a means to entertain dignitaries, suppliers,
and distributors, just as she and my grandfather had.

By the time I was born in 1959, my mother and father had settled
into life at Grant's Farm. My earliest childhood memories, of course,
are of them waving at adoring crowds as they made their way through
the grounds—both were beautiful and charming and had the world at
their feet. We didn't have a typical parent-child relationship. It was understood that the brewery and running the farm and all other aspects of
the business came first. That meant in so many ways that we children,
while enjoying the finer things in life, didn't experience a traditional
upbringing. But I didn't know that, because I had no comparison, no
other way of life. I thought simply, *This is how every kid in America lives.*

At the end of each April, we opened Grant's Farm to the public.
Children from all over would come to feed our hundreds of baby animals: goat kids, foals, even baby bear cubs. We watched as tulips and
daffodils made their way out of the ground and blossoms burst forth
from the trees. The Cardinals returned—both the birds and the baseball team my father owned as he watched over their spring training
in Florida. Everything ran its course. I came to understand that with

every new beginning came an ending. So long to the cold and lonely winter, hello to the warmth and all the people who made their return. Everything made so much sense to me back then. I could smell the newness in the air and the trees. I could hear the peacocks' and elephants' calls. Everything heralded the return of life back to Grant's Farm. I couldn't wait to hear the tram announcer describing the area to visitors. I loved hearing it from my bedroom window. To this day, I can still feel the rush of anticipation when I heard these sounds—the intense desire I had to run and put my boots on and head out to see all the action. I couldn't wait to go to work on the farm with all the farmhands whom I considered friends; their children, some of whom were my best friends; and the various animals whom I grew to love.

When I say I was baptized on this land, I mean it in the most literal sense. When I was born, my father gave my mother, a Catholic, the gift of a small chapel on the grounds in honor of my birth, even though my father wasn't Catholic at the time. I was baptized—and spent every Sunday—in that chapel. Eventually, at my mother's urging, my father also became a Catholic in 1971. He was baptized in the same chapel, as were my two younger siblings, Andrew and Christina, as well as all of my children.

He had the chapel dedicated to St. Hubert, the patron saint of hunters. My father, an avid hunter, was enamored by the story of Hubert, one he had grown up with. His grandfather Adolphus had built a chapel that was also dedicated to St. Hubert on his California estate, Ivy Wall. Hubert was a man devoted to his first wife, but after her death, he retreated inside himself and set off to the forest to hunt. One day, while in pursuit of a stag, the magnificent animal suddenly turned, and between his two antlers was a blazing crucifix. There are lots of versions of the story, but one version has the stag talking to Hubert about how to regard and respect animals—namely to only shoot them with clean shots so that the animal does not suffer. Additionally, one should only shoot animals past their prime and never a mother with her young nearby. According to the legend, the stag told Hubert, "One must forgo a shot for a trophy." As a result, St.

Hubert is known as the patron of sport hunters and is said to be the
father of ethical hunting behavior. In so many ways, I was baptized
into the love of and reverence for animals.

However, while my father was an avid huntsman and revered animals, he was not above mounting or using animals as trophies. He
learned the practice from his father, who mounted everything he killed
or found. We even had two carrier pigeons that he mounted. The mo-
rality of killing animals back then was not what it is today, and nobody
at the time thought they were going to go extinct. When he shot them,
carrier pigeons were so plentiful that they filled the sky, their shadows
darkening the earth. To this day, we have natural history museums begging us to sell or lend the taxidermied carrier pigeons to them, because
nobody thought about mounting them back then.

My father, like my grandfather, mounted everything he found too.
When he found a dead white owl, he mounted it, and now the white
owl is almost extinct as well. He even mounted the first African elephant
born in captivity at Busch Gardens in Tampa. Unfortunately, water had
seeped into the area where the baby elephant was just born, and it caught
pneumonia and died. He kept these animals out of respect, curiosity,
and to keep a memory of the nature he observed.

One story my mother loved to tell is that back when she was dating
my father, an orphaned baby English stag they called Ike fell in love
with her. She bottle-fed him when he was first born, and he imprinted
on her. Wherever she went, he followed. My mother was a veritable
Snow White. Animals flocked to her. At one point, Ike grew a large
rack of antlers and became too large, powerful, and protective of my
mother. So my father released the stag at Belleau Farm, his hunting
lodge located about forty-five miles northwest of Grant's Farm on the
other side of the Missouri River. The stag managed to leave Belleau,
swim across the Missouri, and eventually make his way back to my
mother on Grant's Farm! One moonlit evening after a party, my father
drove my mother through the Deer Park. The stag saw my mother
in the car and started to ram it with his antlers, trying to get to her.
He was so intent that he was lifting one side of the car completely off

the ground. My father finally had to pull out his pistol, roll down the window, and shoot him. The next day, my parents went out to the Deer Park and found Ike dead. My mother's favorite way to end this story was always, "The stag wanted to mount me. But we ended up mounting him." Even though she was a good Catholic girl, she never lost her sharp sense of wit.

We took in a lot of rescue animals for rehab and to live out their lives in quality, and animals were often a gift for us children. While we were in church on Easter Sunday, the Easter Bunny would leave baskets outside. We would all get our baskets and then run to the pond to go Easter egg hunting. Once our baskets were full of eggs and chocolate, we headed back to the Big House. There we would find baby bunnies and chicks temporarily dyed all sorts of colors. My mother, for all of her quirks, was someone who knew how to make children happy. While she often seemed cold and distant, especially as we grew older, the magical holidays often made up for it.

It was clear to all of us children that my mother had a deep love for three things: God, her home country of Switzerland, and all of nature, animals included. She instilled that deep reverence in each of us. She designed the church to look like the ones she attended in the Alps. She had the chapel blessed by a local cardinal, and every Sunday local priests—Fathers O'Riley, Wilkerson, and Duggan—would arrive to say a private Mass for us and whoever was visiting the farm that day. Often, Mom and Dad would invite friends and businesspeople over, and afterward we would all return to the Big House for a breakfast feast. All the adults would sit around the large table on the main floor, and we children would sit high up in an alcove of sorts, a *Katzentisch* that overlooked the adults below, as they did in the homes of fine Europeans. We ate there with our nurse, Yolanda.

We were never permitted to participate in the adult discussions below. Our job was to sit "and be good little children." The butlers would serve us breakfast—big trays of eggs, bacon, sausage, potatoes, and German pastries. We were content to be fed and in each other's company. Below at the dining table, my honorary relatives Uncle Jack and Aunt Marie, Sunday staples, talked to my parents. The table was often filled with "uncles" and "aunts"—not all really relatives, but adults who frequented our house and who my parents considered their closest friends. In addition to being a good friend of Mom and Dad, Uncle Jack worked at the brewery, as did Uncle Frank Schwaiger, my godfather and my dad's brewmaster, but neither was a biological relative. After breakfast, the men would jump in my father's Mercury Morris, which had no doors, and they would shoot "chippies"—sparrows or other birds that had overpopulated to such an extent that Dad thought they needed thinning out.

Often, Sunday was a workday for my dad—there were never really any days off. Business associates would come, and the conversation would center on the business. My mom's job was to look beautiful and be charming and supportive of my father's ideas. Of course, the real family was there too. Both my first cousins, Aunt Lammie and Aunt Puddie, would often come with their husbands, Uncle Herb and Uncle Willis. Aunt Puddie was born in the Big House in 1915. One person who wasn't typically in attendance (with the exception of Thanksgiving and Christmas) was August III, my half brother. He wasn't raised Catholic, so it made sense that he didn't attend Mass. But he never joined us for brunch either. I suppose he wasn't interested in spending time with his father's third wife and their new family. He would have been in his twenties at the time, busy learning the business in preparation to be my father's successor and raising a family of his own. They had three children, but in 1967, when I turned eight years old on August 22, August lost his newborn son, Michael, who shared my birthday. It must have been a tragic loss for him, his wife, and their other children, August IV and Susie.

———

We kids were often left in the care of the staff. I recall one time, when I was very young (probably three or four, because our nurse then was Anna, and she left before I turned six), waking up and crying in the middle of the night because my parents had taken all my older siblings to Disneyland without me. It was common to leave children who were too young at home with nannies. I don't remember how (or *if*) I was calmed down that night; I just remember being a child and knowing my parents weren't home—and that they wouldn't be home for some time. I also remember being so upset because we all watched my father's "friend" Mr. Disney on the television, and I was sad I didn't get to go and meet him. But that's just the way it was. Today Christi and I wouldn't dream of leaving a child behind. But by the fifth kid, I guess my parents were used to doing things that way. Especially in the spring, when they would spend a month or two in Florida to entertain guests on his boats and attend spring training for the Cardinals—without us.

Though spring was beautiful at Grant's Farm, there were several times in my childhood that we celebrated Easter in Florida at our beach house. While my parents were away and we children anxiously anticipated Easter, our train ride, and seeing our parents again, the staff would ready the Big House for their return. Spring cleaning was in full swing. The carpets would be rolled back and vacuumed. The floors would be polished until they shined. Everything would get a fresh coat of paint too. Every time I get a whiff of paint or Pine-Sol, I am transported back to those days. Everything needed to be maintained in tip-top shape for my father's exacting standards when he returned. My mother's decorator would usually come by and point out areas that needed refreshing—new curtains or furnishings—and things would be replaced to keep everything looking beautiful.

And it wasn't just the house that needed to be "refreshed." Joseph, one of our longtime butlers, would help Yolanda bring our old spring clothes down from the cedar closet on the third floor. We each took turns trying on hand-me-downs. When things didn't fit, we'd pass them on down the line. Even though we were from a wealthy family, we didn't waste clothing—or much of anything, for that matter. We didn't go on shopping trips every year; we shopped our closets instead. It was a European, old-fashioned way of doing things—very much the way my mother did things—so that's what we did.

I found it all fun. I remember trying on my shorts, swimming suit, and short-sleeved shirts and practically wiggling in my skin from the excitement, knowing that we would be headed down to Florida and we would see our dad and mom after a long month without them. The best part was traveling by the Adolphus, our private railcar which they hooked to the passenger trains. Before I was born, Dad had lent the Adolphus to Harry Truman to travel on while he campaigned for the presidency. Dad also used it a lot in the fifties to travel around the country when Anheuser-Busch fell behind Schlitz in sales. He visited every wholesaler to rally them and recapture the number one spot (which he eventually did). I didn't know any of that as a kid though. I also thought every kid had their own train car. Still, it was always so exciting.

Our mom, or sometimes both parents, would take the train back to meet us and bring us down to Florida. I remember our chauffeur driving us children to Union Station, and then we boarded the train midafternoon. We'd travel all night and the next day. Though I am a bit fuzzy on other details, I recall unhooking from the passenger train somewhere in Tampa and then attaching our railcar to a small engine that would take us the rest of the way. By the second morning, the train would pull right into Busch Gardens. I vividly recall seeing bright green grass and palm trees.

We were always the caboose of the passenger train. Our parents allowed us to stand out on the balcony at the back of the railroad car as we were leaving the train station to wave goodbye to everyone. Once the train reached thirty miles per hour or so, my mother would gather us back into the big living room, filled with couches and chairs. From there we walked back into the dining room with a table that could seat about twelve people comfortably. In the next section of the car were the bedrooms. I always stayed in the bedroom that had bunk beds. I recall at least one nurse stayed with us younger children. There was another room for the older kids and a master bedroom for my parents. There was also a kitchen and serving quarters with two bedrooms for the butlers, servants, and the tutor. It almost seems surreal to write this. This wasn't the 1860s, but the 1960s—and it was my life. Though it feels like a million light-years away in some respects, it also feels like it was just yesterday.

I remember so distinctly looking out the window and watching things seem to fly by. I'd lie in my bed, staring out a giant window, and watch the passing lights and countryside. It was such a beautiful way to fall asleep—hearing the *chug, chug, chug* of the train, like a soothing drumbeat, lulling me to sleep. When we awoke and the train made stops, my mother would let us get off and explore with our nurse and tutor.

Since school was still in session, the older children would be home-schooled by the tutor so we could stay in Florida longer. Though, it didn't much help—some of my siblings were held back a year because we spent so much time in Florida and they missed too much school. Because my dad never had much use for formal education, he never seemed to be bothered by it. He was more concerned that we kids had a good work ethic and knew how to behave—which we all did, especially on these extravagant trips.

Eventually, as I got older, we upgraded from railcar to private jet. We flew to Miami, and we would meet our mother and father there. Before we arrived, they used the yacht, *A & Eagle*, to entertain their friends and guests. They would occasionally sail it over to Palm Beach and dock there. The high-end designer shops on Worth Avenue such as Akris, Altona, Amina Rubinacci, Bottega Veneta, and many more would open at night specifically for Mom, Dad, and their guests for private shopping excursions. When we arrived, there may have still been guests on the yacht, and we would take the *A & Eagle* back over to St. Petersburg. Over the course of five days, we would travel through the Okeechobee Water-way, where we would see alligators and wildlife everywhere. I can still see my dad, with his sailor hat and a cigarette hanging from his mouth, carefully steering the 120-foot ship through the narrow Okeechobee Canal and watching the alligators snap and descend under the water.

I loved being on the *A & Eagle* with all my siblings, Mom, Dad, our nurse, the staff, and my favorite chef, Rollins, and butlers, Frank and Warren. They were such great guys whom we loved like brothers.

They let us play blackjack with them. Rollins dealt, and he was the luckiest son of a gun I ever knew. As he dealt, he would crack us up and be so entertaining that we happily turned our money over to him. It was always money well spent. We all loved each other and were like one big family. In my mind, we were all having the best time. I don't recall any sadness or any fighting. One of the butlers commented to my mother one night about how lucky he felt to work for our family and said, "You have the happiest family in the world." We weren't poor little rich kids—unhappy, lonely, or sad. We didn't think our parents were distant or neglectful for leaving us for months at a time; we simply didn't know any different. We loved our nurses and butlers. We loved our life together. We loved every experience our father and mother created for us. It was impossible not to.

We took the yacht to see spring training and baseball games. We also had the little runabout boats that we would take out to go waterskiing. When we weren't boating, Mom and Dad were entertaining. Dad always threw himself a massive birthday party on March 28. He would invite all his friends and a lot of businesspeople and celebrities—Frank Sinatra, Ed McMahon, and more baseball greats than I can count. We would have the finest oysters and shrimp and all this wonderful food brought in, and we would all feast.

We also got behind-the-scenes tours of Busch Gardens. We could hang out with the elephants and see animals right up close. Dad was always with us, and I recall everyone on staff giving him their undivided attention and respect. "Yes, sir, Mr. Busch, sir. Right on it, sir." We were never alone on these outings with my mom and dad. Many times there were other people there too, as their guests, who were somehow related to brewery work, so it was understood by all of us children that we had to be on our best behavior—we were always being watched and judged. I was so happy to be there, I couldn't help but be on my best behavior. I loved being around the animals—and my mom and dad, even if I knew they weren't paying attention to me. Our nurse Yolanda was in charge of the discipline, so we knew never to misbehave in her presence; she was always nearby on those excursions.

While our days were spent mostly with our nannies and the staff, at night my mother would come into our bedroom and say our prayers with us before bed, give us a kiss, and tuck us in. In the morning, my brother Andy and I would wake up early to find the best shells that washed up on the beach before they were taken by other seashell hunters. Then we would head over to the boathouse, where the captains and their crews were busy scrubbing down the boats. We would get to drink coffee with Dad's secretary, Margaret. We felt like adults.

Late in the morning, Mom would wake up and sometimes make us go with her on her long four-mile walks up the beach. She did this twice a day while we were in Florida. We had to be little "troopers" and do as she said, so we trudged along. Walking, swimming in the ocean, and being outside was an important part of her health and beauty routine, and we were all just along for the ride—or walk or swim—no matter how long and painful it was. While I wasn't crazy about those walks, I did enjoy being with her. Those times were few and far between. In the evening after dinner, when she wasn't entertaining, we would walk the beach again as it got dark. Once, we stumbled upon a body, which freaked us out until we realized it was made of sand!

We rarely saw our father during the day, as he was often busy with the business and running the Cardinals. However, we had a special time with him too. On occasion, we accompanied him to the baseball games, and he invited us back to the locker rooms. The players would give us handfuls of bubble gum, and we kids stuffed our pockets with them. It's funny what you remember: all the baseball greats were right at our fingertips, and I remember the giant jars of bubble gum and just being able to pal around with my dad. It's truly the little things in life that are memorable.

It was always sad to say goodbye to Mom and Dad when it was time to go back, but I loved returning to the farm as much as leaving it. I couldn't wait to see all the guests start arriving. I always missed the staff and their children, who became my friends. I also loved all the work that preparing the farm for the opening day of the season entailed. Most of all I loved welcoming all the new baby animals being born. A wonderful liveliness burst through the air. By the time we arrived back in late April, sometimes with our parents and sometimes not, the redbuds, crab apple trees, and magnolias would be in peak bloom—like our family. The Cardinals were on the verge of becoming one of the biggest teams in the United States, Budweiser was world-renowned and a household name, and we Busch kids, the third bumper crop, had the run of Grant's Farm. All was well in the world.

I realize I had a completely different childhood than most people. But in so many ways, I was a kid who loved animals, springtime, spending time with my family, as well as baseball, travel, and adventure. It seemed like it would never end, especially with summer just around the corner.

Chapter Five
SUMMERTIME

Despite the relative distance between our parents and us kids, I've always said my mother and father provided an amazing childhood for us. There is no word to describe it other than *magical*—though a more appropriate turn of phrase would be *magic show*. Because, while it was magical, it was by and large *for show*. My mother loved entertaining and made every single event she hosted a spectacle. She took great pride in hosting dignitaries and famous people—Yul Brynner, Danny Kaye, Bob Hope, Henry Fonda, John Wayne, Frank Sinatra, Ricardo Montalbán, Peter Graves, Arthur Godfrey, and many others. But perhaps the pinnacle of the parties she threw was her famous *Camelot*-themed auction and fashion show.

As a young boy, I lived for magical nights like the *Camelot* party. My mother spent months preparing the Bauernhof for it.

The Lerner and Loewe musical *Camelot* had come to the Muny Opera House in St. Louis in June 1969. Everyone was talking about it, and Camelot parties and events were all the rage that year. My mother had the idea to re-create Camelot on Grant's Farm. The Bauernhof had an open courtyard with a large fountain in the center, so it provided the ideal spot. It was already styled to look like an old European village, so it made perfect sense. The Bauernhof was surrounded by several connected buildings—including the horse stables and carriage house as well as offices, garage spaces, the concession stands, and the dairy house / butcher's shop. Since more than five hundred dignitaries and famous people—baseball greats, actors, and actresses—were invited, my mother wanted the area to be spotless. The Big House was too small to accommodate all the guests, so—for one night—she converted all the other areas, including the horse stables, into elaborate rooms so they could comfortably hold everyone in addition to the auction items and fashion show. A large runway was erected. Massive floral arrangements and candelabras were brought in and covered every table and available space. Andy Williams was hired as the entertainment. She spared no expense. Most of the guests were coming in from out of town, and every room in the Big House was occupied. (I had to move to a bedroom on the third floor, as my room was commandeered for guests.)

On the night of the event, we children were dressed in our finest. Though we weren't invited to the party, my mother allowed us to open the main door to the Big House and greet the local guests. After the party got underway, we snuck out of our rooms and entered the Bauernhof; as long we remained out of the way and no one noticed us, my parents didn't seem to mind. I recall going up to the VIP apartment with my friend Alex Georges, who was the son of Bill and Marilyn Georges, the Houston A-B wholesaler and great friends of my mom and dad. We peeked in on the guests who were drinking, smoking, and having a great time. Then we headed over to the main event. There we saw gorgeous women dressed in elaborate gowns. Most of the women looked like Jackie Kennedy, a fashion icon of the time. The former first lady had given *Camelot* a renaissance of sorts since she mentioned that her husband had loved the musical.

My mother, a Catholic who spoke many languages, considered herself a woman of culture in the same class as Jackie. She wanted to create a similar air of regal elegance at Grant's Farm that Jackie had brought to the White House. My parents had become good friends with President Lyndon B. Johnson and Claudia "Lady Bird" Johnson by that time. They spent a lot of time with them on President Johnson's ranch in Texas, where they liked to hunt. And, of course, the Johnsons came to Grant's Farm as well. Since my mother saw her husband as a leader in his own right, she saw herself as a first lady. And she wanted to celebrate the life they'd created as royalty would—or in this case, as close to royalty as one can get in the United States.

At some point, the nurses made us come home, and just like that, the magic show ended for us. We were sent back up to our rooms. Our nurses made sure we were tucked into bed with lights out while our parents carried on into the wee hours of the morning. I don't remember the cleanup, but I imagine it was extensive. The guests all left, and life went back to normal.

As I grew up, I began to notice that my father's absences had extended. He wasn't home much in the summer because he traveled a lot. And it wasn't just for work either. He had always been an avid sportsman and traveled to horse shows all over the country with my brother Peter. He owned both hunters and jumpers. My father had several professional riders for his horses who traveled with him. My mother didn't share his enthusiasm for traveling around the country to horse shows, although she showed horses and won numerous ribbons herself. When he was in town, occasionally he would invite us out with him to Cardinals games. We would sit in the Red Bird Roost—our private box high up in the stands. We kids would watch the game intently on the outside balcony. I was ten years old by then, and I knew the batting averages of every hitter and the names of every player. My father rarely sat with us but instead would play Gin and Honors (a card game) with friends and business associates inside the Red Bird Roost. My mother wasn't a fan of baseball either, so she wouldn't accompany us. We were usually chaperoned by our nurses, and our chauffeurs would wait outside for us.

The more I think about my childhood, the more I realize how small a role my parents played in my day-to-day life. When we were at Busch Stadium, we pretty much had free run of the place. We could go to the dugouts and the concession stands and anywhere we pleased.

Back on Grant's Farm, we woke hours before our mother did, who by this time was becoming increasingly dependent on sleeping aids and pills to wake her up in the afternoon. We spent our days hopping trams, playing with all the animals, and riding our horses and the sheep. We pretended we were cowboys. We would run up to the hayloft and swing on the big ropes. As a parent now, I cringe at the thought of it. It was dangerous, and any one of us could have been seriously injured at any time.

We learned a lot at a young age, and we grew up fast. I was chewing tobacco at eight and smoking cigarettes before I was ten years old. At the time, the farmhands were allowed to go to the dairy room and drink as much beer as they wanted. Some of these guys would quit for the day at four or five in the afternoon and stay until nine o'clock at night, drinking beer for free. Then they would head to a tavern right up the street from Grant's Farm, the Ten Mile House, and continue drinking. I don't know how some of those guys made it into work by six thirty or seven o'clock the next morning, but they would always be back to do the whole thing all over again. I knew all of this because I would be hanging with them during and after work *and drinking beers with them*—even at ten years old, although I wasn't too crazy about the taste of beer back then. (Of course, it would have been a "Cardinal" sin if that had gotten out.) Back in those days, the workers were even allowed to drink beer during their breaks. It was just the way it was. I felt so grown-up and like I belonged. The nurses only asked that we make it home for lunch and take a nap each day in the summer, so we hung out with the farmhands, then headed back for our daily nap. So much for being a grown-up!

Every June was spent largely outdoors seven days a week. We'd have about five thousand people coming through Grant's Farm six days a week. One of my jobs was to take care of the baby elephant, Tina. I'd walk her around and let the public pet her. When we heard the bell ring, we knew it was time to head home from wherever we were on the farm.

On many occasions, as soon as my father arrived home from work, he and my mom would take us out in the horse and carriage. My dad mainly drove a four-in-hand of Hackney horses, but there were times he drove teams of mules, Gelderlanders, and several other breeds of horses. Many times while coaching, we would shoot the black pigeons because Dad hated to see them crossbreed with his prized white ones. Frank, Dad's loyal valet who worked with him for more than forty years, used to joke that my dad was racist for shooting only the black pigeons. They would always get a big kick out of that joke no matter how many times Frank told it.

We also often brought a .22 birdshot gun with us in case a rogue buffalo got the herd mad enough to chase us. The birdshot wouldn't kill or even injure the buffalo, but it would usually sting enough to turn them the other way. When this happened, it could be pretty precarious, even deadly. Dad was always able to outrun the buffalo and get the horses in control, sometimes with the help of our stable hand. My dad was an amazing whip, and that fact saved us from certain disaster, I am sure.

It wasn't rare to be chased by animals in the Deer Park, whether we were coaching or riding horses. It was not uncommon to be bucked off or run away with by a spooked horse. The buffalo, rheas, elephants, camels, elk, and llamas would often scare the horses, and we would be in for the ride of a lifetime either on a horse that was bucking or bolting off with us. After a horse ran off with my sister Trudy in the Deer Park, she rarely rode again. There was a lot of danger that somehow we miraculously lived through.

I'll never forget one time when my older sister Beatrice was riding a horse called Happy-Go-Lucky through the Deer Park. It was very muddy, and Happy-Go-Lucky went right into the mud and started pawing at it. Beaty was kicking and screaming to get Happy out of the mud, but Happy liked it so much she decided to roll around in it while Beaty continued to scream and shout, begging her to stop. By the time the horse stood up, she and Beaty, who was now crying because of her hurt pride, were completely covered in mud. It was the funniest thing any of us ever saw. I just remember how happy-go-lucky my father was that day. I can so clearly see the huge smile and hear the joyful laugh the scene brought out of him. It's something I've never forgotten.

In the evenings, we'd have dinner with my mom and whoever she was hosting. If Mom and Dad were home together, and they weren't entertaining (a rare occasion), we'd sit out on the porch and have dinner, which always consisted of black radish, white asparagus, fresh tomatoes, and rhubarb—all grown in our garden and faithfully tended to by our gardener, John. During dinner, we'd listen to the baseball game.

As the sun set and it got cooler, all the animals would come out of the valley's woods to the higher land of the Deer Park to graze with their newborn babies. From our view on the terrace, we could see animals grazing on the vista out in the Deer Park. Dusk was always such a beautiful time. After our dessert of rhubarb sauce, we'd take a drive around the farm.

When my mother hosted elegant parties on the terrace, the guests could look out over all the animals. My parents would even have a parade of animals out on the front lawn for more than one hundred and fifty guests. During the cocktail hour, the workers from the farm would bring camels, parrots, llamas, Clydesdales, chimps, macaws, bears, elephants, and even Dad's priceless hunters and jumpers, who were the top horses in America. As the band played the great hits from Frank Sinatra, Louis Armstrong, Burt Bacharach, and Herb Alpert & the Tijuana Brass, the guests were able to interact with each other and the animals as the sky turned from dusk to dark.

As the stars came out, the guests would be ushered inside to the dining room for a three-course meal. The butlers would have set the table with the finest china and silverware before their arrival. On each table there would be beautiful silver-and-gold vases, overflowing with gorgeous seasonal floral arrangements. The band would move inside and set up below the main staircase in front of the elegant Tiffany window, which was installed by Tiffany himself. The stained glass window depicted a bucolic scene with an English stag and was one of the most striking features of the giant foyer. No matter what time of day you happened to look upon the window, some new detail would emerge. It's hard to overstate just how grand and romantic these hosted events were.

We children were never allowed to eat with the guests. During parties like this, we ate dinner in our private kitchen on the second floor, and then we'd be tucked in early by our nurse Yolanda. As night descended, I'd watch thousands of lightning bugs fill the sky and would fall asleep to the faint sounds of my father's favorite song, "The Girl from Ipanema."

If we were in town for the Fourth of July, Bob Baskowitz, the president of the bottling department, would put on an epic fireworks display just for us in our front yard. It was the type of display one might see at a downtown or riverfront celebration. My parents always hosted a large party. I remember one Fourth of July when I was very young, I became frightened by the loud sounds and ran inside to find Loretta, who was one of the housekeepers. I often sought solace from the people that worked for us, never once thinking to go to my parents for such things as affection and comfort, even though they were often sitting right beside me. Loretta held me close and said, "Don't be afraid, you know that's not going to hurt you." Her reassuring words and the warmth of her hug instantly made me feel better. I went back outside and watched the rest of the fireworks, and I wasn't afraid anymore.

We spent some Fourth of July holidays in Cooperstown, New York, when we visited my dad's sister, Aunt Pummie. She was a real character and a joy to be around and reminded me so much of my dad. She inherited some of her properties from my great-grandfather Adolphus, who went to Cooperstown to escape the extreme St. Louis heat. She also owned a wilderness area and, like my father, opened it so the public could enjoy it. It consisted of museums, animals, and a couple of Clydesdales. But what I loved most was the real locomotive that she owned, complete with a straight mile-long track. I spent hours riding it down to a playground and back again. While we were there, we often stayed in her lake house. We enjoyed taking her boat, the *Chief Uncas*, out on the lake.

As a child secluded on Grant's Farm, I didn't have access to life outside our bubble. Like in the movie *Elf*, when Buddy the Elf leaves the seemingly "magical" North Pole and enters the real world, that is where the real magic begins for him. The thrill of discovery—and all the richness and complexity of the real world and its real inhabitants— exists *outside* the bubble. We kids were all somewhat naive about how the world worked and were ill prepared for it. This became abundantly clearer as I grew older.

We spent two holidays in Switzerland with my grandmother, who owned an apartment building in Lucerne and lived in one of the units alone since my grandfather had died. One year Peter and I were sent to Lucerne for six weeks to stay with my grandmother—or Grandmommy, as we would call her. We traveled there on our own, without any adults, and that in itself was an experience for a ten-year-old. When we weren't with our grandmother, the two of us would ride our scooters to the train station in Lucerne and watch all the trains come and go. We also went to the Flora Garten, where we ate cheese fondue and watched Alfredo the Comedian, who later became internationally known, perform his many comic antics. We spent a lot of time alone with my grandmother's maintenance man, Mr. Phister, who let us smoke cigarettes and cigars and drink wine with our lunch.

It was truly the first time we lived outside the "North Pole" bubble. In St. Louis or St. Petersburg, and especially on Grant's Farm, everyone knew us. And if they didn't know us, all we had to do was mention our father's name, and everyone most certainly knew us then. It was definitely different in Switzerland. One day Peter and I went off on scooters through the town and got lost. After some time, when it was clear we had no idea where we were, Peter and I went up to strangers and asked them where our grandmother Frau Buholzer's apartment was. They looked at us like were insane. They didn't know who we were or who Frau Buholzer was. We were stunned—literally stunned. We kept repeating our names and our grandmother's name. As if that would have made a difference! Eventually we found our way back, but it was definitely an eye-opening experience for me. I believe it was the first time I realized that people who were not Busches lived quite differently than we did.

One Fourth of July, my mother and father sent Peter and me to a ranch camp in Colorado. It was only supposed to be a month-long session, but my mother and father weren't ready to have us back, so they called and asked the camp to keep us for *an extra two weeks.* The camp was closed, so our counselor, Fred, took my brother and me, loaded us in his hippie van, and just drove us around the country with him. We were homesick at first. We were just children, road-tripping with a stranger. We were smoking and drinking with him too. I don't think our parents had any idea what we were up to. It somehow seemed perfectly reasonable to them to leave their kids with a random stranger.

After a while, I got quite used to living on the road and having my fill of cigarettes. It was a fun adventure when all was said and done. And by the time we got back, I was sad it was over. I cried in my mother's lap because I missed hanging out with Fred so much. Mom said, "Billy, you can go back any time you want." That helped me get over my sadness instantly. My mom was so understanding. Instead of getting mad, she completely empathized. It made me realize in that moment that I didn't want to leave home. My mom could show a lot of wisdom at times, and she could even be comforting, though there were plenty of other times when she would become volatile when I would share similar feelings with her. You really never knew what you were going to get. I always had trepidation and had to be on guard. But this time, she seemed to know what to say.

In August we usually spent a couple of weeks or more on Belleau Farm, the shooting lodge on the other side of the Missouri River. It was a different environment at Belleau; namely, it was a real working crop, cattle, and pig farm. Of course, the entire staff would come with us. In the mornings, Rollins would make a giant breakfast for all of us and the workers, and we would all eat together. Then we would work on the farm all day. It was a huge operation, and I learned to drive big tractors and heavy equipment of all kinds. The days were hot and strenuous. Dad would always have projects to accomplish and work for us kids to do, whether it was to vaccinate the cattle, castrate the pigs, or drain and clean out lakes. He was just like John Wayne in cowboy movies, his favorite actor, barking out orders as we also rode horses and worked the cattle herds. Dad would always say, "I haven't had a day off in more than twenty years," because even when he wasn't working at the brewery, he had the farms to manage and take care of.

Still, we'd find time to swim in the lakes or go waterskiing with the sons and daughters of the people that worked and lived on the farm. They were our friends. We did a lot of frog hunting and fishing there. We would also shoot snapping turtles and bring everything we caught or shot back to Rollins, and he would cook it all up for us. We would have frog legs, fish that we caught out of the lake, and turtle soup most nights of the week. Rollins also fried up the pig testicles, which were called Rocky Mountain oysters.

It was here that my oldest brother, Adolphus, and I learned how to play polo. Polo was one sport Dad loved to watch his sons play. He played polo as a younger man, and he told us the story about his friend Tommy Hitchcock, who was the greatest American polo player that ever lived. Dad's claim to fame in polo was having played with Tommy. He and Tommy often went duck hunting together, and Dad told us about the many times he watched Tommy suffer from convulsions and fits—he would shake uncontrollably for several minutes at a time after hearing gunshots. According to my father, he suffered from some sort of PTSD (though it was not called that at the time) or brain injury, which he most likely incurred during World War I as a fighter pilot as well as from serious crashes he took while playing polo.

I never got into equestrian jumping or hunting like my brother Peter did. My dad hired some of the best trainers in the world to come out to the shooting lodge in the summer to train my mom, sisters, and my brother to get them ready for the big horse show that Mom and Dad hosted at Grant's Farm in the fall. We would all go on riding excursions together as a family, and even little Christina, the baby of the family, would ride along with us. She had two horses to choose from, Nipperdee and Princess, and both took such good care of her and never did anything wrong. Because of them, Christina rode with all the confidence in the world. She was a little thing, but she was also a tomboy and did her darndest to keep up with all of us. Even when we herded cattle, she was right there along with us. At just six years old she was helping to herd our registered Angus cattle. She exuded spirit and spunk.

As much as I played with the farmhands' and workers' children, as I grew up, it started to become clear we were living very different lives—that we were different from most families. The bubble of perfection seemed to be leaking. Not everything was magical. The summer I was ten, my brother Adolphus was out riding with his friend Jeffrey on Grant's Farm. On their way back, heading to the barn, they had to cross a bridge. Jeffrey's horse slipped and fell, and Jeffrey's head came crashing down hard onto the side of the bridge. An ambulance was called to the farm, and he was taken away. We were all incredibly shaken. We all rode horses every day, and though we'd fallen before, we'd never seen someone fall from a horse and not be able to get up.

My mother called Jeffrey's mother immediately. She said, "Jeffrey has had an accident."

I could make out Jeffrey's mother saying, "Oh, he'll be fine." I am sure she thought it was just like a previous call she had received from my mother when Jeffrey fell and broke his arm while playing at Grant's Farm.

But I saw something in my mother's eyes that I had never seen before. And my mother didn't lie to the woman. She didn't reassure her. She became very grave and matter-of-fact, saying simply, "No. It's not what you think. It's much worse. He's unconscious, and they took him to the hospital." I had this completely empty feeling in my gut at that moment. I was so scared. Jeffrey was my friend too, and we had all played with him and his family. We knew them all and were very worried.

Two days later, Jeffrey died. We were all devastated. It was the first time I knew someone who had died, and it was a fifteen-year-old child with his whole life ahead of him. My mother showed very little emotion.

She was a tough woman and didn't break easily. I, however, was shaken. But unlike the fireworks, where I could run to a housekeeper and ask for a hug, I had no one to talk to or explain what I was feeling. The emotions just sat there, heavy in my gut with no place to go. Sure, we'd had our brush with accidents on the farm. One year, when I was very small, one of the trams had jackknifed out in the Deer Park, and people on the train were badly hurt. One person even lost an arm. But no one had died. While it was terrible and frightening at the time, in many ways, we felt like we'd been spared the worst. Jeffrey's death was different. It hit everyone hard.

By the time I was a teenager, I was much more aware that the bubble we were in wasn't so much leaking but had completely burst. My mother and father were spending much longer extended periods away from us children—and each other. My father was off at horse shows a lot more, and we know now with much more certainty that he wasn't being faithful to my mother on his trips away. My mother always claimed that my father was having an affair with Marie, a close friend of theirs who often came with her husband, Jack, to our happiest-family-in-the-world Sunday Mass and brunches.

My mother was struggling with a number of physical and psychological issues. For a time, we children were even told that she may have a brain tumor. She would spend six weeks at a time away from us. While it was true that is what she *thought* it was, it wasn't in fact a tumor after all. It really boggles my adult mind that we were told (and left to worry) that my mother may have a brain tumor rather than being told the truth.

The truth was, I found out later, she was in rehab in Switzerland, trying to wean herself off the drugs she was addicted to that helped her sleep and wake up. At one point, she even tried shock treatments to help with her psychological issues. We have reason to believe she was also getting face-lifts and other treatments, for which Swiss doctors are well known, but was too proud to admit it. She may have even been having an affair, though I don't know that for certain.

While our parents were off with their respective paramours at horse shows and rehabs in Switzerland, we kids were left in the care of nurses and chauffeurs for most of the summer. We still kept a similar schedule even though our parents weren't with us. And when August came around the year I turned fifteen, we headed, as was customary, to Belleau Farm with all the workers and their kids.

One night while we were sleeping, a stable hand came and knocked on the door of the shooting lodge and woke us up. He was obviously panicked. He explained to us that our mother's favorite horse, Sultan's Sign, which had won numerous ribbons, had somehow escaped from his stable and was missing.

We kids ran out of the house in the middle of the night and joined the stable hands searching the grounds for our mother's prized horse. Eventually, we found poor Sultan severely cut up from a barbed wire fence that he must have gotten himself tangled in. He was covered in blood. It was a grizzly scene for all of us children to take in. *My God*, I thought to myself. It was simply horrible. We had to call the vet to come right away. The horse was carted away and had to be operated on and treated for his serious wounds.

It wasn't as though I had a premonition at that moment, staring down at the beautiful steed—a speckled silver-gray majestic specimen, fit to be ridden by royalty—struggling and gasping for life. I knew my family was not what it used to be and that things were changing, but I had no idea at that moment we would never be a whole family again. I didn't know that one of my siblings would not return with us to Belleau the following summer—or ever again—and that her death would tear our family apart. Nor did I know that our parents would never again be the happy, carefree, dancing King Arthur and Queen Guinevere of their very own court. No, it only became clear to me many years later, as a grown man looking back on my childhood, that what happened that horrible night was indeed a sign.

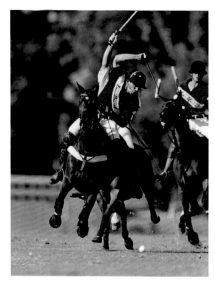

Me playing polo on the
Bud Light team in 1999.

Family photo, 2021.
From left to right:
Peter, Grace, Abbey,
Gussie, Christi, Billy
Sr., Maddie, Haley, and
Billy Jr.

Family photo.
From left to right:
My elephant Tina,
me, Adolphus with
his cockatoo Cocky,
Andy, Christina, Beaty,
Mom, Beaty's goat
Bud Girl, Trudy,
our camel George,
and Peter.

My Dad, Gussie, with his elephant, Tessie, at Busch Gardens in Tampa Florida, 1971.

Gussie (Dad) and Trudy (Mom) on Christmas in the Big House at Grant's Farm. Happy times underneath the mistletoe in early 1960s.

Dad and Mom's wedding reception in Hot Springs, Arkansas (March 22, 1952).

Mom and Dad at a dinner party, circa 1955.

Dad at the brewery showing off the new Budweiser bottle that came out in 1970—called the "stubby," this was one of the first twist-off cap bottles.

Dad boarding the Adolphus railroad car at Union Station, circa 1950.

Dad whooping it up in the Roaring '20s.

Dad inviting Saint Nick in the Big House after his long walk up the hill from the Deer Park.

Dad waving his red Cardinals hat to the adoring fans at Busch Stadium in one of the three World Series the Cardinals played in the 1980s.

Dad at the St. Louis brewery with the Budweiser eight-horse hitch—his marketing brainchild.

Dad with the Cardinals he had just purchased in 1953 to help sell more Budweiser. Notice Cardinals great "Stan the Man" Musial in the background, standing to the left.

Dad with President
Lyndon Johnson,
circa 1964.

Dad on the right with
his brother, Adolphus III.

Dad with his famous protection dog,
1915.

Dad and Mom and the employees at a Grant's Farm Christmas party.

Dad with sons Billy (left) and Andy (right).

Dad with the animals at Busch Gardens in Tampa, Florida.

Dad with President Harry Truman at Grant's Farm, 1950.

Colonel August A. Busch Jr. atop Dalchoolin, 1945.

August A. Busch Jr., founder of The Bridle Spur Hunt Club and Master of the Fox Hounds.

Dad with Red Schoendienst and Stan Musial.

MR. AUG. A. BUSCH AND SONS.

August A. Busch Sr. with sons (from left), Adolphus and Gussie, on horses.

August A. Busch Sr. and his favorite hunting dog.

August A. Busch Sr. driving his elephant, Tessie.

August A. Busch Sr. driving the sleigh in the snow at Grant's Farm.

Me atop a horse on the Bud Light polo team.

Christi and my wedding at the Grant's Farm chapel, 1991.

Me coaching with my parents (sitting on Mom's lap).

Me on the Bud Light polo team taking a shot.

Me training elephants, Bud and Mickey, at Grant's Farm.

Dad and me.

Me with Mom, Trudy, and sister Beatrice, circa 1961.

My Halloween party, 1965.

Buffalo in the Deer Park on Grant's Farm.

Christina and parents at The Schlachtfest 1974.

Christmas decorations at Grant's Farm.

Christmas with the family, 1967. Front, left to right: Andy, Mom, Dad, Christina, and Peter. Back, left to right: Adolphus, Beatrice, Trudy, and me.

Clydesdales at the Anheuser-Busch brewery stables in St. Louis, Missouri.

Grant's Farm Deer Park with the Big House in the background.

Our private chef, Rollins, at Schlachtfest 1974.

Saint Nicholas at Grant's Farm.

Saint Nicholas party. From left to right: Beatrice, Trudy, Dad, Peter, Adolphus, Mom, and me in Mom's arms.

The Big House at Grant's Farm.

Mom and little sister, Christina, in 1967.

Ulysses S. Grant's cabin.

Chapter Six
FALL IN CAMELOT

At the end of summer, we headed back to Grant's Farm and to school. Unlike most kids who piled onto buses, our chauffeurs drove us every day and picked us up each afternoon. Over the years, I became incredibly close to one chauffeur in particular: Nathan Mayes, a tough guy from the city. After I got out of school, we would have to wait until my sisters got out from their all-girls school. While we waited, we would play and throw the ball around, or we'd just get out of the car and hang out. He'd chase me around, always making sure I was having fun. We became really good friends over the years. In many ways, my best friends and mentors were my chauffeurs. I now realize this made me a bit of an oddball at school.

As I got older, I became more aware that I was different. And my peers let me know it. I faced my fair share of bullies in my day and not just at school—also on the farm and even at camp. For a long time, I just thought that was how it was for a kid like me. For example, when I went to the Colorado River Ranch camp with Peter, we were assigned a cabin with about six other boys and a counselor. When I arrived, I laid my bag on a bed. I didn't put much thought into it. Then some kid came in and said, "That's my bed."

I simply said, "Okay, well, there are other beds over there."

The kid wasn't having any of what he perceived as my entitled atti-tude. "No, that's *my* bed," he said.

I was confused. I didn't understand what was happening, and he just hauled off and punched me square in the mouth.

I didn't fight back, probably because I was so stunned. But, in some ways, I was kind of used to it. Peter, my very competitive brother, fought with me all the time. It was typical brother rivalry. Not only was he bigger, but he was also intimidating because he was three years old than me. I was no match for him. Even before that incident at camp, I'd had some other run-ins with bullies. When I was at Grant's Farm on a field trip with my class (many schools took their classes to Grant's Farm), I took all my buddies up to the concessions to give out free candy and popcorn.

A kid from another school on his own field trip came up to me and said, "Give me some candy!"

He wasn't my friend, so I said, "No, I don't know you, and I've given all I can to my friends."

Again, he told me he wanted some candy, and without warning, he punched me.

By the fall of seventh grade, I guess you could say I was sick of being punched. I was also sick of being taunted in school. Because I spent the majority of my days with farmhands, I had developed a country accent. I was often called a redneck hoosier. But that kind of name-calling wasn't what bothered me. There were other names that cut deep. One day when Nathan came and picked me up from school, he could tell something wrong.

He looked at me when I got in the car and said, "Billy, what's the matter?"

"Nothing. Not a big deal," I said, trying to shrug it off.

He wouldn't let it go and looked me square in the eye and said, "Listen, you'd better tell me right now. What's the matter with you?"

"Well, there's this guy in school, and he's always, you know, calling me a *rich pussy*. I don't know what to do." Even though I could handle being called a redneck, this kind of insult bothered me the most.

I could tell Nathan was upset by this. "This is what you do, Billy," he said. "The next time he walks by you and calls you that, don't ask any questions. You hit him in the face as hard as you can. You've got to do it really quick. You hit!"

"I can't do that!" I said.

"You listen to me," Nathan said gravely, "this is how you're going to take care of things. You hit him as hard as you can."

He wanted me to learn how to stand up for myself and stop being bullied. I trusted him implicitly and knew he had to be right. Nathan cared a lot about me and wanted the best for me. I promised him I would try.

Sure enough, the next day I went to school, and as I was walking through the hallway, the same kid walked by me and said, "You rich pussy." I looked around because I was about to do what Nathan told me to do. But I stopped myself when I saw a teacher and some of the Benedictine monks who ran our all-boys school nearby. I knew I would be in serious trouble if I punched a kid in the hall. I knew how this worked: no one would care that the kid called me names. I would be in trouble for throwing the first punch.

Knowing this, I leaned over and said, "How about you and I step outside?"

He looked at me quizzically. He wasn't expecting a response from me. "What?" he asked.

I repeated my question because I had every intention of walking out that door and doing exactly what Nathan had told me to do.

Seeing how serious I was, the kid got really nervous and said, "What's the matter?"

I kept calm. "Nothing. Just come on outside."

We both started heading for the door, but when we got there, the boy put his hands up and started walking backward, saying, "Bill, Bill, what's the problem?" Of course, he knew what I was going to do. I realized right then, I didn't even have to hit the guy to stand up for myself.

When I got in the car that afternoon, I told Nathan what happened. "Nathan, I've got that taken care of. I don't think that guy is ever going to call me names again." He had a big smile on his face and was so proud of me. He was the first person who ever taught me how to stand up for myself, and I loved him for it. It came in handy too, because there was no shortage of people who underestimated me or felt like because of my name they could make fun of me.

That kid never called me a rich pussy again, and it didn't take long for him to become one of my friends. Nathan had gotten it right.

Another, older kid on the playground said basically the same thing. He was the biggest kid and in the grade above me. But this time no teachers were around, so I did exactly what Nathan said to do in those situations. I hit the guy. I hit him so hard that we both went down. He was so shocked; the fight didn't last too long. But all my friends were around us and saw it. They were cheering me on because he was an incredible bully to everyone. I took care of that. Before Nathan's advice, I wasn't really a fighter at all.

Nathan always had my back, and he didn't just protect me from the bullies at school. It was quite common for the household staff to beat the hell out of us kids too. For the most part, my parents allowed it; they didn't seem to be bothered by it. Joseph, our German butler, had a really bad temper. It didn't take much to make him angry. He would get extremely violent when he got mad and would sometimes beat us up. I would never let anyone who worked for me ever lay a hand on my kids. But in those days, that was acceptable. The staff had free rein to discipline us physically, and in Joseph's case, this was whenever he was in a bad mood or had too much to drink. One day I must have said or done something that upset him (though I have no recollection of what), and Joseph came at me and started beating me up. Even Yolanda, who herself was known to hit us from time to time, felt it was too much and tried to come between us. She was yelling and screaming at Joseph to stop, and she tried to pull him off me. She kept screaming, "Stop! Stop it, Joseph!" I am sure she thought he would kill me.

This all took place on a Saturday, Nathan's day off. When Nathan came back to work on Monday, Yolanda told him what Joseph had done and how violent he had been with me. When I got in the car that morning, Nathan asked me about it. I said, "It's okay. It's no big deal. He just got pissed off. That's just how he is."

Nathan looked at me again and said, "No way, man. In no way should anyone touch you like that. That should have never happened." I could tell he was really pissed off. I didn't say anything else.

When I got home after school, Frank, my dad's valet, told me that Nathan had grabbed Joseph and pinned him up against a wall. He had him by the neck and said, "If you ever touch that boy again, so help me God, I'll kill you."

It scared the hell out of Joseph. Later Nathan said to me, "Billy, if that man ever does that to you again, you come get me. If I'm not here, you go into the chauffeur's room where we store the sports equipment and you grab a baseball bat. And you hit that motherfucker as hard as you can. You got it?"

My father had never said or done anything like that for me. No one had. As I said, my parents had no problem with us getting the shit kicked out of us by employees. In many ways, we were like lambs being led to the slaughter, completely unprepared for the real world. Nathan gave me the real-world training and backup none of the other adults in my life could. That's why all of us kids were so close to a lot of the people that worked for us. They were our mentors in a lot of ways.

That all being said, even though Joseph had his moments, he wasn't so bad. There were a lot of times he was the greatest guy, and we had a lot of fun with him. He would come down to Florida with us, and he took Andy and me to the carnival. He took us on the bumper cars, and we had the best time with him. He always told hilarious jokes. Everyone knew that his really bad temper came out when he drank too much. We all knew to prepare for it because when he got drunk, he had a tell: he would start walking on his tiptoes. If we saw him serving us dinner on his tiptoes, we knew he had been, as he used to say, "sampling the beer on tap to make sure it's cold."

Even he and my dad would get into it with each other once in a while. Dad fired him once, but he hired him back because he couldn't find someone to replace him. Joseph worked so hard. He was there six days a week and worked eighteen-hour days. And that was nothing for someone like him. He'd serve us breakfast, lunch, and dinner. He'd clean the entire house, the dishes, and polish the silver. He knew the inner workings of our house better than anyone. He even counted all the light-bulbs on the first floor—some ten thousand. He loved telling people how many lightbulbs he had to check, shine, and clean. He could get away with beating us here and there because he really was irreplaceable. My dad valued work ethic above all else—and I mean *all else*. Luckily for me, I had Nathan looking out for my well-being and safety.

It wasn't only the staff that looked out for me—even the elephants came to my defense on occasion. When I was eight or nine, a couple of my buddies from the farm and I were hanging out and running around by the creek. Even though I went to a private school, it was about twenty-five miles from the farm. Back then, all the kids that lived around Grant's Farm went to public schools. So I spent my days with them. My friends recognized a few bullies from their school also hanging around the creek, and they started exchanging words. The bullies were shout-ing at us from the bottom of the hill, and the next thing I knew, they started running after us. There were probably six of them and three of us. As we took off running, my two friends headed one way. I was so scared, I didn't know where I was going. When I looked back, all six of the kids were chasing me. Like Forrest Gump, I just kept running! My only thought was, *I'm going to run over to Tessie.* Tessie, my favorite ele-phant, and I had a great connection, and she always showed incredible affection toward me. She was staked out on a chain under some trees. I was breathing like a son of a gun by the time I reached her.

Tessie looked at me, and I could tell she was completely alarmed and worried. Immediately, she took her trunk and pulled me close to her. Then she saw these boys coming after me, and it dawned on her that they were chasing me. She gently let me go, moved me out of the way, and started to trumpet and make growling, roaring noises. She kept trumpeting and shaking her head, all the while flapping her ears. She was kicking up her legs, and dust was flying everywhere. As soon as the kids saw Tessie standing between them and me, it took them half a second to realize they weren't going to be able to mess with me. They just turned around and took off the other way. Tessie came back, put her trunk around me, and pulled me close again. She started making these wonderful whistling sounds that are the sounds of affection a mother elephant might make to her calf. Long before Nathan taught me to stand up to bullies, Tessie protected me and fought my battles for me.

But all the bullying came to halt when I decided that I needed to get strong and start working out. I had become really sick of being picked on and having to defend myself constantly. Like I said, I wasn't only picked on by the people who worked for us and by my peers, but by my older siblings as well, especially Peter. It was nothing too terrible, just normal sibling rivalry. But he definitely targeted me if he got pissed off, especially if we were competing and I happened to win. One day I was flipping through a magazine, and I saw a picture of this kid on the beach getting sand kicked in his face by some bigger kid. Next to it was another picture of the same kid transformed. He had become big and strong because he lifted weights. It was an advertisement for a weight set at Sears. I told myself right then and there, "I'm going to get that. And no one is going to pick on me ever again."

The only problem was the set cost eighty bucks. I was about twelve or thirteen at the time, and I didn't get an allowance and didn't have a job yet. So I went to my dad and asked for the money, but he would never just hand money over to us. He said, "If you want the money, you will need to pull the weeds out of the pasture." *It was a six-acre pasture.*

So every day when he came home from work, he'd inspect my attempts at weeding. It took me about three days to do it perfectly. When he was satisfied, he gave me the eighty dollars, and I gave it to one of the guys who worked for us. I showed him the picture in the magazine and asked, "Would you go down to Sears and get this weight set for me?"

As soon as I got it, I took that weight set down to the basement. I read how to work out in the instruction pamphlet that came with the set, and it said to work out three days a week, never more than that.

So I worked out religiously and eventually got bigger and stronger. The first one to realize that I was gaining more confidence and getting stronger was Frank. One morning when we were getting ready for church, I was putting on my tie and Peter was there with me. The next thing I knew he started to get rough and tried to beat me up. I grabbed him, put him in a headlock, and punched him in the face. I couldn't believe it. But no one was more surprised than Peter. After that, Frank came up to me and said, "Pete ain't going to be messing with you anymore. You've been down there working out. I've been watching." And he was right. Peter never touched me again.

By the time I was thirteen, I was pretty strong for a kid my age. It became clear I would be able to make the football team. Nathan was always throwing me the ball, but now I also had the body of an athlete. I went out for the football team, and I learned quickly that I was pretty good. Nathan and Frank loved football, so they took me under their wing and supported me. They followed my progress and watched as many games as possible. I often asked them how I was doing, and they'd tell me and help me.

In the seven years I played football, including college ball, my father only made one game. Frank told me that he was going to get my dad to come to a game whether he liked it or not. Our football field sat in a valley, with a parking lot on top of the hill. It was off-limits to drive down from the parking lot to the field. But, in the second quarter of this particular Saturday afternoon game, I looked up from the field of play and saw my father's Mercedes slowly making its way down the hill. It was great knowing Dad finally made it to a game. I, however, wasn't proud of the score. We were down twenty points. A few minutes later, I saw the Mercedes heading back up the hill. When I got home after the game, Frank was sitting at the kitchen table.

"Thanks for bringing Dad out, but why did you leave so soon?"

Frank replied, "Your daddy asked me what the score was and I told him you were losing twenty to nothing. And he told me, 'Come on, Frankie, let's get the hell out of here.'"

I had to laugh, even though I was disappointed that the one and only time my dad came to my football game we were getting our butts kicked. And that was the extent of my dad watching me play football. Meanwhile, Nathan would watch every practice and even give me pointers.

When I think of the fall, I can't help but think of Nathan, Frank, and football. And, of course, the farm. I loved Grant's Farm this time of year. Throughout my entire childhood, it was the *one* constant. The farm would anchor me and remind me of all the traditions and what was good and beautiful about life. No matter what was going on at school or with my friends, siblings, or my parents, I could count on the farm staying the same. I guess you could say it supported me like Tessie, Yolanda, Nathan, and Frank did. I could always count on it to be the same, season after season.

In the fall, we would start shutting it down for the season, and the public would stop coming. It was the time of year when the farm was just for us—the family and the workers who ran it. The sad part always was saying goodbye to Tessie and the elephants, who would head back to Busch Gardens in Tampa to avoid the harsh Missouri winters. The days became shorter; we could no longer spend hours every night out on the terrace. If it was still light when we came home, we kids would head out and pick up all the buckeyes that fell from the trees that were turning shades of bright gold, orange, and red. The air was crisp and cool. But as the weeks went on, the days got shorter still. Often by the time Dad arrived home from work, it would be dark. As night descended, we could hear the sounds of the elk bugling from the Deer Park. Since it was too dark to go coaching with the horses and there was no public to entertain, my dad would come home, take a hot bath, and come down for dinner in his pajamas. He would always have on a robe and beautiful slippers. Most evenings, he and Mom would sit in the gun room in front of the big fireplace and have a cocktail and appetizers.

At dinner, we would have a three-course meal in the beautiful dining room, sitting in front of a roaring fireplace. Christina always sat to the right of Dad. It was so clear to all of us that she was indeed the apple of his eye, his "Honey Bee." She could do no wrong in his eyes. One night she very casually looked up at him and asked him to open his mouth. When he did so, she reached in with her fingers and pulled out his false teeth. If anyone else had done that, they would have been in trouble, but Christina had a way with Dad. He just laughed and laughed. Christina melted something inside him no one else could. This was true even on the coldest of nights, when the chill that lingered between Mom and Dad was palpable, both of them now merely tolerating each other as my dad was growing older and my mother was enjoying the prime of her life.

Like the drafty, cold, and old castle we lived in, the atmosphere was made icier by the stony silence between my parents. But the air was warmed with the help of the roaring and popping fireplace and the youthful laughter and chatter of us kids. Somehow those nights seemed to thaw even the hardest of hearts, and for a brief moment, I felt that I could hold on to what once was and what could be; that somehow things in the family could be like the farm: go through their cycles but remain the same; that, like all the times before, we would come out of this icy winter together.

Occasionally in the fall, my mother would host dinner parties, especially when it helped the company. When the head hop buyer from Germany or one of the heirs of the Anheuser family, who owned a lot of Anheuser-Busch stock, came, my parents would put on quite a show for them. They would be dressed in their finest and be on their best behavior, and all of us kids would be asked to do the same.

Halloween was a great time of year too. I loved how our house was always decorated. Giant pumpkins were brought in and adorned the front of the Big House. My parents would arrange to have a haunted house built (also called the Spook House), made of straw bales, where we crawled through the tunnels. Some years, we were allowed to have Halloween parties and invite our classes from school. And all the kids got to go through the Spook House. Then we would all hop on the train and go through the Deer Park.

My mother would always go to New York and buy us all wonderful costumes. On Halloween day, Frank would drive our whole family to Uncle Jack and Aunt Marie's house nearby. We would go trick-or-treating and then have dinner. Usually, Harry Caray, the famous sports announcer, and other guests would be at the party. After the party, Frank would drive us directly to the shooting lodge, Belleau Farm, as the duck season opened on November 1.

Instead of being twenty-five miles from school, we were now forty-five miles away. That meant longer drives with Nathan in the morning and afternoon, which I never minded. By the time I started high school, my days at the Benedictine school were much longer. We weren't dismissed until five o'clock in the afternoon. By the time we got back to the shooting lodge, it would be six. Even if it was dark, we kids would head out on our bikes. We loved to hang out with Dick, the son of the shooting lodge manager, Clarence, and his wife, Kate, who also worked for us. They raised six children on our farm. And all their sons worked on the farm at one time or another.

The shooting lodge was on the migration flyway for ducks and geese heading south for the winter. They stopped on the farm's lakes to rest on their way to warmer climates. Every evening we watched and listened in amazement as thousands upon thousands of geese took flight from the rest lake and flew right over our house to spend the night on the river, honking a cacophonic chorus. They looked like giant arrows traversing the moonlit night sky. Early in the morning, their honking was like an alarm clock, waking us for our long drive back to school. This was nature at its finest, and why I love the Midwest so much to this day.

Dad loved the migration too. I never saw him so mad as the time when my brothers Adolphus and Peter took their rifles one evening and shot into the flock of geese as they flew back to the river. Shooting geese with rifles and after sunset were against the law. Dad, first and foremost, very much respected hunting regulations and strictly made sure we all followed the rules. He also knew that shooting at them in this way would mean there was a good chance they would not return and he would no longer be able to watch the migration. Dad would only allow hunting geese at the end of the season, which was just before we headed back to Grant's Farm. Needless to say, when Dad found out, he humiliated them in front of everyone—the entire family and all the workers on the farm. He had this booming voice that was so intimidating and loud. Everyone knew that he was pissed. The public shaming was so harsh, it never happened again.

I shot my first duck with Dad on those lakes. I was about twelve years old. He took me out one day even though I had the flu and a terrible headache. But Dad loved a tradition. He took each of us kids out in the marsh at Belleau to shoot our first duck, and afterward he would mount it. Today was my day, sick or not. Out in front of us, a duck landed on the water.

My dad shouted at me, "Shoot it!"

"Dad, I can't shoot it," I said. "It's sitting on the water." I didn't tell him what I thought, which was that it's not very sportsmanlike to shoot a duck just sitting on the water.

He screamed back at me, "I don't give a goddamn! Shoot!"

So I did. It was a spoony.

He sent our retriever dog, Jigs, out to get it, and when the dog brought me back the duck, Dad said, "I'm proud of you. See there, pal, you got your first duck."

Not long after that, a mallard came flying in, and with my newfound confidence, I shot that one too. A mallard was a much nicer shot than the first, and I said, "Hey, Dad, let's call this one my first duck instead." If I was going to have a mounted duck, I wanted it to be a mallard that had not been sitting on the water. And sure enough, he did that for me. I still have it to this day.

We spent the whole month out at the lodge, but my favorite event was always the giant *Schlachtfest*, which was the German word for the ceremonial slaughter of pigs and the subsequent feast. It was a tradition in Germany for private households or inns to celebrate the end of the harvest with such a festival. In Germany it was common for the family of the slaughtered pig to invite neighbors and friends to partake in the feast. Never ones for subtlety, my parents went all out for this event. It was massive. The last year we all celebrated the *Schlachtfest* together, I was fifteen. My parents invited nearly five hundred people out to the lodge. They hired a German band and built a giant bonfire that everyone could dance around. Oxen were brought in from Grant's Farm to pull a giant oxcart fully decorated with giant Bavarian pretzels and all kinds of German sausages hanging from hooks to be delivered to the guests. The pigs were slaughtered and hung the day before. Then the sausage makers would arrive at the lodge at four in the morning to get the fire going and the water boiling. The meat was ground through a giant meat grinder, and the pig's intestines, which were used as sausage casings, would be strung out to be stuffed. Sausages of all kinds were boiled in giant cauldrons that hung over wood-burning fires, just as they would have been in ancient times.

In the evening, when the guests arrived, they were greeted with giant German steins filled with the famous Munich dunkel beer, which my father had made at the brewery specifically for the *Schlachtfest*. Everyone would drink their weight in beer. There were also little gin stands all around so people could drink a German gin called *Steinhäger*, which was meant to keep you warm. There was singing and dancing around the bonfire while the German band played the oompah music. "Ein Prosit" was always my favorite song. Later in the evening, after dinner, a rock-blues band would come in and play, and everyone would dance until early in the morning.

I can't believe how much we all drank. I learned young and in a hurry not to drink too much of the *Steinhäger*, because it would get you. I knew I didn't want to pass out or sleep through the party like my brother Andy and a couple of my friends did. The party would last all weekend, and the fire would stay lit for days. After the party, many of us would stay behind and keep stoking the fire. There was a sense that we wanted the party to last forever.

But things couldn't last forever. The *Schlachtfest* signaled the end of a season, and 1974 would be the last time all of my father's children would be together, and the last time we would celebrate this event. I was a freshman in high school. My father, at age seventy-five, was still the king of the court, though his reign was about to come to a startling end. My mother, nearing forty-seven and at the height of her beauty, was holding fast to her queendom, as vivacious and spirited as ever. She was well into her second affair. But for a brief moment, we were all together, laughing and celebrating. For one magical weekend, we were transported back into the wonderous snow globe. I can still see little Christina laughing and being her sassy self, enjoying the limelight as the youngest child. I can see my cousins and friends wrestling each other off the dock and trying to throw each other into the frozen lake. All of us kids were having the time of our lives.

Before we headed back to Grant's Farm, all the guests would leave, and we as a family would prepare for Thanksgiving. My half siblings and all my nieces and nephews would come back to Belleau. Rollins would cook us a delicious Thanksgiving feast. Frank, Joseph, Yolanda, Nathan, and Warren would all help out. Most of my older half siblings would give toasts and speeches. August III, one of the most incredible speakers I've ever heard, always focused his speech on business. On that last Thanksgiving together, he announced how Anheuser-Busch was meeting and exceeding all its expectations—selling twenty-five million barrels, a record. My father beamed with pride for the brewery's success, as well as all that his oldest son had accomplished under his watch. Whenever Anheuser-Busch reached a goal like this, he would give us each little pins or medallions that marked the milestone: 10 Million Barrels, 15 Million Barrels, and 25 Million Barrels. We all collected them and shared in my father and August III's pride.

On that day, I thought we were going to make it as a family. Everyone seemed to be getting along. The season seemed to remind us all of what really mattered—our traditions and each other. I had never felt better. I was getting bigger. I wasn't being bullied anymore. I was on the football team. Life was looking up.

I couldn't wait to get back to all my friends. Before we left for Belleau, my friends and I had converted a goat house into a party house. We called it the Goat Shit House because when we found it, it was covered in goat shit. We cleaned it out, painted it, even ran electricity to it, and made it our clubhouse. We had incredible parties on the weekends there. Hundreds of public school kids would come to them. For the first time in my life, I had more friends than I could count. I couldn't wait to get back. And the first week of December was always my favorite because with it came the Feast of St. Nicholas—one of my favorite days of the year.

That Thanksgiving I had no idea that in a few days, my entire life would fall apart. That it was the end of the Busch family as we knew it.

Chapter Seven
THE END OF CAMELOT

My father, who was already inundated with work, always found the end of the year to be especially busy. This was particularly true in 1974. Even though he had recently stepped down as president and a longtime friend and colleague, Dick Meyer, now held the position, he was still working as hard as ever. As CEO and chairman of Anheuser-Busch, he was also trying to manage the relationship with his oldest son, August III. It came as a real blow to August III that my father handed over the reins of running the company to someone outside the family—that had never been done before. Even though August III had been preparing for the leadership position for years, he was only thirty-seven, and my dad didn't think he was quite ready for all the responsibility that being a president entailed. Dad needed a very seasoned, mature person in that position, and Dick Meyer, who had been an executive with the company since the year August III was born, was the guy, not August. Though Dad had to get approval from the board to elect Meyer as president, it wasn't difficult. Board members usually go along with the recommendations of the CEO, and beyond that, the board respected Dad's leadership ability and many of them were family members.

August III was an intense and competitive person. I am sure this didn't sit well with him, especially since he was witnessing what we all were at the time—my father beginning to show signs of wear. The stress of being chairman and CEO, training a new president, managing his son's feelings, and ensuring his legacy was clearly getting to him. He was still working seven days a week and trying desperately to keep Budweiser at the top as the number one US beer company.

The toll this had taken on my father had never been more visible than during the massive shareholders' meeting in St. Louis that same year. At seventy-five, my father, a once gregarious and gifted public speaker, suddenly suffered from stage fright. His nervous system was clearly affected, and he struggled to speak in front of crowds. He was so worried about this particular meeting that he prerecorded his speech and planned to lip-synch it in front of the large crowd. When he got up on stage and began to speak, my mother, siblings, and I were so embarrassed for him. We were all watching him lip-synch—completely off count from the prerecorded speech. All of us were cringing in our seats. But it wasn't nearly as bad as when he was awarded the very prestigious Globe-Democrat Man of the Year. As he accepted the award, his body and voice shook violently. He was shaking so badly, he couldn't control his arms. The entire podium he held on to rattled. I couldn't watch it. What made it worse was knowing how incredible he had once been in front of everyone. It pained me to see him this way.

To add insult to injury, my father had a number of other concerns. There was the obvious one—his marriage was failing—but he had grave concerns about the economy and his family's welfare as well. At the time, there was a gas shortage. With gas prices surging, my father felt it was important that we use a more fuel-efficient vehicle. He purchased a Volkswagen van to transport all of us children back and forth to school. There was absolutely no substance to this vehicle. It practically had no front end, and riding in it was an adventure, to say the least. (We used to joke that it was a "coffin on wheels.") In addition, my father was incredibly worried about another topic dominating the news at the time: Patty Hearst's alleged kidnapping in

February of 1974. This had long been a serious issue of concern for the Busch family that dated back to when he was much younger. His nephew, Adolphus "Buppie" Busch Orthwein, son of his sister Clara, was kidnapped by a masked gunman on New Year's Eve 1930, and it must have stuck with him. Though the boy was returned unharmed and without incident and the kidnapper went to prison, one of my father's great fears was something similar happening to his own children. Terrified of losing one of us, my dad hired an armed bodyguard to travel with the chauffeurs and us children wherever we went—and that Christmas was no exception.

While it was always clear to us that our dad loved us so much that he would go to any length to protect us, my mother loved us in the only way she knew how—by celebrating holidays in the most outlandish ways possible. In her mind, she thought that if she made everything look perfect, nothing could possibly touch us. She was adamant about passing on her European traditions. Despite my parents' marriage troubles, that year the holidays felt no different. My mother took great care to make sure the Christmas season was festive for us children, regardless of what was going on between her and my dad. All the halls were decked. All the trees outside on the lawn were lit up. The house was brimming with wreaths, Santas, reindeer, and ornaments. Every morning in the Big House, each of us children woke up and opened our personal beautiful European advent calendars in our rooms—counting down the days until Santa came.

The biggest of all the traditions she brought to Grant's Farm was celebrating the Feast of St. Nicholas on December 6. This was the night on which St. Nick himself would arrive at Grant's Farm to "check in on us." Mom always told us Santa was all around, "watching" our every move during the holidays. While we had armed bodyguards escorting us to and from school, when we were in our house, we had the spirit of Santa observing us day and night. Santa wasn't just this jolly old man but, rather, a strict disciplinarian. He was someone to both fear and respect. And he wasn't just coming to Grant's Farm to see if we were on his naughty or nice lists. No, the Santa my mother taught us about would throw you in a sack, take you back to the North Pole, and make you toil in his workshop if he caught you doing anything wrong! At fifteen years old, I knew he wasn't going to do that to me. I was too big and knew at this point that it was impossible. Still, all those "cool teen" vibes went out the window the second we heard Santa's bells while we sat with our parents in the gun room waiting for his arrival.

Santa always parked his sleigh in the Deer Park (of course) to let his reindeer eat with ours. All of us children would wait and wait. The anticipation would nearly bring us to the brink of collapse. I remember lifting Christina up to the window when she was five or six to see if she could spot Santa's lantern in the distance and feeling her little heart beat so fast that I thought she might explode from all the anticipation and fear. Then out from the Deer Park, Santa would suddenly appear in the dark night, walking toward the Big House with his lantern in his hand and his sack swung over his back. In his other hand, he'd carry a large switch made of sticks. When he finally made it to the terrace, the doors would swing open, and Dad would invite him in. Santa would set his lantern down and walk inside, handing the switch to my mom and saying, "Use this if the children misbehave." He'd make his way to the big couch and sit down, and each of us would talk to him. He'd ask how each of us had been. He'd take out his big bag of presents and give us nuts, oranges, and candy canes. I'd easily forget I was fifteen in those moments. It was so fun to believe. It was still such an exciting time. Since we always had school that day, I'd be so excited all day long. I couldn't wait to get home, change into my pajamas, and wait alongside my siblings, especially my two younger ones—Andy and Christina—who still absolutely believed in Santa in 1974.

On that St. Nick's Day, Nathan waited for our bodyguard, who always accompanied him on our rides to and from school. For some reason, he was late that day. Nathan delayed as long as he could but didn't want Andy and Christina to be left outside in the cold waiting. He had to pick Christina and Andy up from their separate grade schools, drop them off at home, and then immediately turn around to pick me up from my high school after basketball practice let out so I could make it home in time for all the holiday festivities. It was a busy night, so he hopped into the Coffin on Wheels and headed out.

When practice got out at five o'clock, it was already dark and cold. I paced and wondered, "Come on, Nathan! Where are you?" It was so cold, and the gym had already been locked for the night. I was waiting and waiting, and no one came.

Suddenly, one of my friends got out of his mother's car and came up to me and said, "Billy, we just heard on the radio that there was a pretty serious accident. It might have been someone in your family. I think you need to call home."

Since the gym was locked up, I walked a quarter of a mile from the gym to my high school and called home. My godmother, Aunt Marie, answered. This was unusual. She wasn't the first person I expected to hear on the other end. She said, "Oh, Billy! Where are you?"

"I'm at school," I said, "waiting for Nathan."

"Billy, you stay right there. We're going to send somebody to pick you up right away. Just stay right there."

I was shocked to see the farm manager, Ed Pike, pull up. He had worked for our family for years but was not a chauffeur. I had no clue what was going on, and he didn't tell me much. All he said to me was, "Billy, expect the worst and hope for the best. I'm taking you to St. John's Hospital. Christina is in critical condition, and Andy's in serious condition."

"What about Nathan? How's Nathan?" I asked.

"Nathan was killed in the accident."

I don't remember feeling anything in that moment, and quite honestly, not much after that. It was as if I was frozen inside. I remember the words. I remember hearing Nathan was killed . . . and it's like something turned off inside me. No tears. No emotion. In fact, I don't remember how we even got to the hospital. But suddenly, there I was, standing in the St. John's waiting room. I saw my dad—he was just crushed. His body was lurching forward. August III and Dad's secretary, Margaret, had gathered around him and were comforting him. I was so confused. No one said anything to me. My father didn't speak any words to me. I looked around and couldn't find my mother because she was with Christina. Yolanda and my sister Trudy were also in Christina's room. Neither Yolanda nor Trudy left Christina's side.

Then someone came out and said, "Come on, Billy. Come and see Christina."

When I heard Ed say that Andy was in "serious condition," for some reason I thought he was in the worst shape. I thought Christina was going to be okay, so I was wholly unprepared for what I was about to see, and no adult was in the right frame of mind to prepare me. Just a few moments before, I had learned that one of my best friends and mentors had been killed, and now I was walking into my sister's hospital room. I expected to see her little cherubic face—the one I would see light up at the window when Santa was coming. Instead, I didn't recognize what I saw lying there in a coma, hooked up to a plethora of tubes, wires, and machines. Her face was so swollen that she didn't look like Christina. I understood now why my father refused to stay in the room. I didn't want to see Christina like this either.

I left and walked over to Andy's room. I was shocked and relieved to see that he was awake. Though I'd thought he was going to be worse, he was alert, albeit sullen. I would later learn that it was a large truck that hit the van. It crossed the median and crashed head-on into them. The impact was incredible. Andy had been ejected and thrown from the Volkswagen, found several feet away, and made it out with only scratches.

For the life of me, I still couldn't speak. Neither of us could. I just stared at him and he stared back. He was four years younger than me. He was my little brother. He had just witnessed something horrific, and I couldn't reach out and hug him. I couldn't even find the words to ask him, "Are you okay?" The Busch children were never really allowed to let our emotions show—at least not in front of each other and certainly not in front of our mother. I didn't know what to say, what to do, or even what to feel. It was as if a dark veil had descended on all of us. We couldn't see each other; we couldn't see past our own pain.

I know now that I was in shock. My nervous system was completely overloaded, and I just froze. It all felt like a horrible nightmare—like the disembodied dreams where you want to cry out for help and nothing comes out. I couldn't process or make sense of any of it. And the one person I would have loved to talk to at this moment, to tell how heart-broken, scared, nervous, and afraid I was, was gone.

It turns out that the events were even more horrific than I imagined. I learned later that Nathan had been beheaded in the accident. As soon as I heard that, I knew what had happened. I saw it all play out in my mind's eye. I had seen Nathan protect us at least a thousand times. We didn't wear seat belts back then, but whenever Nathan had to brake too fast, he would throw his arms—sometimes his whole body—over to shield us, to protect us from flying through the windshield. That is how I imagine Nathan dying. To this day, in my heart of hearts, I be-lieve—no, I *know*—his last act on this earth was throwing his body over and pushing Andrew out of the way. I truly believe that Nathan saw that truck cross the median and knew it was coming for them and did everything in his power to put his body between that truck and the children. No one had our backs like Nathan did.

Of course, there is no way to know for sure, but it is the only way I can ever wrap my mind around what happened to my friend that day. Otherwise, it would be unfathomable—something impossible to bear. It was a night of absolute horror. I wanted to close my eyes and go back in time—go back to the house, wait for Santa, and forget all of it.

When I walked back out to the waiting room, my father was still there, crying—the only one allowed to show emotion. My mother was still keeping vigil beside Christina and was showing no emotion.

Frank, Dad's valet and Nathan's friend, arrived to take me home.

That night, instead of dropping me off and heading home, he fol-lowed me up to the bedroom I shared with Andy. After I was done brushing my teeth, I came into my room to find Frank on Andy's bed.

"I am going to spend the night with you tonight, Billy."

He didn't say anything else. He didn't need to. He didn't want me to be alone—and I suppose, he didn't want to be alone either. He had lost his friend too.

That night as I tried to fall asleep, I heard him crying, shaking in the bed—beyond bereft. The sadness was everywhere.

The next few days were a blur. I didn't go to school. I remember the fifteen-year-old in me kept thinking, *I hope they get better soon, so I don't miss my basketball game.* It feels crazy and insensitive, but in my teenage brain that made the most sense. I was a kid, and I had no idea how serious any of this was or would be. For eleven days, Christina remained in a coma in the hospital. I eventually returned to school at some point. On December 17, I was called out of class and told I had a phone call.

I went down to the office and took the call. Christina had died.

My parents had made the decision to take her off the machines. By this time, it was well established that she had no brain function and would need a miracle to survive. My father didn't want Christina living hooked up to machines, so he made the call.

A driver came and picked me up. Instead of taking me to the hospital, he took me home. When I arrived at the Big House, I walked into our living room, and Christina's body was laid out in an open casket. I didn't want to look at her. She still didn't look like our Christina, my dad's Honey Bee. It was all too much. And then I saw Rollins, the man who had once said to my mother that we were the "happiest family in the world," kneel before my sister's casket and break down in tears, his whole body convulsing. I wished for all the world I could feel or do something—cry, rage, scream—but nothing came out. I sat there wondering, *Why am I not crying? What's wrong with me?*

Of course, now I know why. I understand how shock works. I understand what the freeze response is in trauma. I also know what it was like to grow up in the Busch household—and never be allowed to share or talk about our emotions. My father had always taught us and his wife not to show weakness and vulnerability. Even though,

when the time came to show such emotion, he was the only one allowed (or able) to show it. The rest of us remained numb. Even Andy
and I never spoke about what happened. In all the years that have
passed since, we never sat down and talked about that awful time.
Even when he was in yet another deadly accident several years later
on the same stretch of highway—and he again survived—we never
spoke of it. No one ever did.

Before we went to bed that night, the monks from my school's
monastery arrived and stood vigil, praying before Christina. And when
I woke the next morning, they were still there—praying. Christina's funeral was held in the Big House; a full mass was said, and she was buried
in the family plot. It was a subdued and beautiful ceremony. My mother
made it beautiful—of course. There were flowers everywhere and chairs
set up in the living room. There was a guard stationed at the door at
certain times of the day to allow family and close friends to come and
pay their respects.

The entire time, my father was beside himself. He could not contain the raw emotion and pain he felt. It was clear to all of us that his
worst nightmare and fear had come true—despite all his efforts to keep
us safe, he had lost one of us. But not just any one of us; he had lost the
apple of his eye, his Honey Bee. He never spoke to any of us about it.
He certainly didn't speak to me or try to comfort me. It was as if Christina's death only affected him—not his children, his wife, or Christina's
friends or relatives. I can tell you for certain that if this happened to one
of my children—and I hope and pray it never does—I'd be putting my
arms around my kids and hugging them and holding them close. I'd
be letting them—encouraging them to—cry in my arms, and we'd talk
about whatever they were feeling 24/7, no matter how long it took for
them to feel better. But in my house, with Mom and Dad, that's not
how it worked. Everyone in the house was in pain, but no one could
talk about it.

The staff was incredibly shaken. I remember Yolanda crying out in
those days right after Christina's accident, "If God takes that girl, he
can go to hell! I won't believe in him anymore." She had been there the

day Christina was born and was as much a mother to her as my mother. Trudy was inconsolable too. She had shared a room with Christina.

My mother, on the other hand, never shed a tear—at least not in front of me. She was so tough—especially on my father. She couldn't abide all of his carrying-on. She screamed, "You know we have six other kids. We have to be strong! Christina is in heaven. We have got to move on!" But my dad just couldn't get over it. It was as if winter never lifted. It descended on Camelot, and just like that—it was over. There was no more happy family. Whatever hope we had that my mother would reconcile or find her way back to loving my father had all but vanished. It was a bridge too far to traverse—between his inconsolable grief and her desire to live.

When Christmas came the week after we buried Christina, my father came down for Christmas Eve in his red coat, but the joyful and radiant smile was gone. He still had the party for his employees, and he handed out their bonuses. We even opened our presents. But there was never going to be the sense of magic ever again, and we all knew it.

Nothing was ever the same again, but the tragedy was far from over. While my father was distracted grieving his youngest daughter, his oldest son—his heir who he had been grooming but whom he hadn't yet made president—saw an opening and a way to push his father out as the leader of the company and take what he thought was his rightful place as the head of Anheuser-Busch. Just when my dad thought he had been through enough and had lost all there was to lose, he found himself in the fight of his life and about to lose it all.

Part Three

BUSCHES' LAST STAND

Chapter Eight
PICK A SIDE

My father seemed to age rapidly in just a matter of a few days. At home, he wept constantly. He just couldn't get over Christina's death. My mother's patience with him had reached its limit. And that impatience gave way to outright anger and vitriol. She was well aware that his behavior wasn't just bothersome to her but that it was getting noticed by his colleagues at work, most especially August III. At dinner, she would scream across the table, "You've got a company to run! You've gotta move on!" Mind you, this was within days of Christina's death. My mom was like the soldier that Dad always wanted her to be—and how we were all taught to be. But Dad no longer was that soldier. Though he had always been a sensitive guy, and in some ways easier to talk to than my mom, he wasn't as explosive with us as our mother could be. While he had a wicked temper, he rarely, if ever, was angry with us kids unless it was absolutely called for. But this was a whole new level of emotional volatility—even for him.

My mother's berating him at dinner just broke my heart. Mom had very little sympathy for him—for any of us, for that matter. She was so full of anger, I think, in part, because she couldn't show her own deep pain and sorrow. She had to be the one to hold it together for the family and for the kids. She wasn't given the time to weep. She was also watching the life she had lived with my father slip away. More than that, she was watching the company and image she helped my father curate get taken from her.

It didn't take long after Christina's death for August III, who also watched my father deteriorate, to argue that my father was no longer emotionally fit to run the company. He basically told the board that our dad was an "emotional wreck." He *was* an emotional wreck, but, even before Christina's death, August III argued my dad was showing signs of unfitness. Namely, he felt he was irresponsible with his spending—his yacht, the *A & Eagle*; all of his fishing boats; his private jets, lavish parties, and entertaining. August III argued that the company shouldn't be paying for these kinds of things. My father was incensed by this.

In the following days, in what amounted to a boardroom coup—the likes of which you would see on the television show *Succession*—August III successfully persuaded his sisters Lotsie and Elizabeth, who had influence with the board, as well as the board itself, which included family members like cousins Jimmy Orthwein and Walter Reisinger, to side with him and oust my father. (Our other half sister, Lilly, refused to side with anyone.) My father was out, and August III was now the head of Anheuser-Busch.

But my father didn't take this lying down. Even though he was bereft over Christina, he still had some fight in him. And my mother certainly had enough fight in her for both of them. In her mind, she had believed that her oldest son, Adolphus, who was also being groomed to run the company, should take over when my dad was ready to step down. But with August III in power, her children and grandchildren would most likely be cut out from ever running the company or even a department of it. Everything she had worked for, all she had cultivated, would be lost.

At a dinner during the days preceding the takeover, my mother's anxiety over the prospect of such an occurrence consumed her. Adolphus was no longer living at the house. Peter and Beaty were rarely around. So it was just Trudy, Andy—who was still recovering from the accident—and me with our parents.

My father, sullen and despondent over the loss of his child *and* his company, was beginning to weep again when my mother looked at him and shouted, "God damn you, you son of a bitch! You pull it together. You can't act this way any longer! Christina's gone. There's nothing we can do about it! And now *that son of a bitch of yours* is taking the brewery from you!"

My dad said nothing. He cried and cried, eventually capitulating, and through tears, he begged my mom to stop her verbal assault. "Jesus Christ, dear. Just stop it. Stop it."

Trudy, Andy, and I just sat there silently watching our parents tear each other to pieces. Even though she was mourning Christina, Yolanda tried to maintain a sense of normalcy for us kids. She could see the tension mounting and saw the writing on the wall, even if we weren't aware of it at the time. She knew the family was crumbling. Andy, just ten years old, was struggling the most. He was suffering from nightmares from the accident and would often get up from his bed at night and leave our room to go sleep in Yolanda's room on the third floor. I would be all alone at night, and I was left to my own devices most days too.

Then one day I came home from school to find my mom gone. She'd packed her things and left for Switzerland to stay with her mother for a while. I am pretty sure she was also having an affair at the time. I don't remember her coming to tell me goodbye or making arrangements for our care. Not that she ever needed to. We had Yolanda, chauffeurs, and cooks. There were no parties to throw, no people to dress up for, no husband to support at the company—so she hightailed it out of there.

Then there were four. Our big happy family of nine was getting smaller by the day.

By day, Dad met with lawyers to see how he could stop the takeover from happening. This dragged on until the early spring of 1975. By then, my mother had returned and seemed ready once again to help my father—and her sons—become the rightful heirs.

Dad said, "We're going to fight this thing." It was clear that by *we* he meant himself and his children from his third marriage since all the others (except Lilly, who remained neutral) had sided with August. My father had one last maneuver to get his job back. He had already made it abundantly clear that we were either "with him or against him." He threatened to disinherit any child who sided with August III. In his own words, they would be "as good as dead" to him. No pressure.

Our shooting lodge, Belleau Farm, bordered a property called Waldmeister, which my father had gifted to August III sometime after my father divorced his mother and before I was born. One day my father called together his sons from his third marriage—Adolphus, Peter, Andy, and me—and sent us out for a throw-down of sorts at the fence line between the two properties. He wanted his sons to "duke it out," fight on his behalf, while he stayed home back at Grant's Farm. In fact, he asked me, at just fifteen years old, to "sock August III in the puss if you get the chance."

I responded, "Yeah, I'll sock that son of a bitch."

We jumped in our Jeep. We were ready for a fight.

But when we got to the property line that separated Belleau Farm and Waldmeister Farm, the gate was closed, because my father had ordered it so. He did not want August III on the Belleau Farm property.

August III had parked on his side of the gate. His nine-year-old son, August IV, was with him, along for the ride, but stayed in their Jeep as August III got out and walked over to the property line.

We pulled our Jeep up, but none of us got out. Adolphus turned off the engine and turned his body toward August III to speak with him. I was relieved to see that August III wasn't packing. I was ready for the worst. We all were. I was mostly surprised that Adolphus didn't get out of the Jeep and that we weren't going to have the opportunity to fight.

We launched in quickly and asked, "How could you do this to our dad? Now? At a time like this! It's just not right."

August III quickly tried to defuse the situation, saying, "I had to do what was right in order for the company to continue to thrive. We had to make this decision. Dad is still affected by the loss of Christina ,emotionally and physically. He doesn't have the strength at this point to run the company any longer."

Unfortunately, we couldn't argue with him, because we saw it too.

We saw with our own eyes that Dad wasn't the same. Though we didn't agree with how August had gone about it—a boardroom coup—we could agree that Dad wasn't the same as he was before Christina's death.

I often wonder what would have happened if I'd followed my dad's advice. If, instead of having a rational conversation with August III, I had gotten out of the Jeep and socked him. I wonder if that would have changed history. I wonder if we'd beaten him, hung him from a tree, or shot him . . . what would have happened to Anheuser-Busch? Would it still be in the family today? Would one of us still be running it? Or would we all be in jail somewhere? Probably the latter.

"You know he was never going to step down on his own. He never would have accepted this. This was the only way I could do it. We'll give him plenty to do. He'll still be president of the Cardinals." August III was all business and reiterated his point. "Listen, guys. Our father is no longer fit to run the company. He is spending too much money. He is not making the best decisions any longer."

There is an old advertisement from the Busch family archives that depicts Custer's Last Stand, and I couldn't help but think we were heading into a battle—the Busches' Last Stand—when we first showed up. But it turned out to be less of a "Last Stand" and more of a "Last Talk."

August III went on and spoke eloquently and rationally. We were shocked. He showed my father an incredible amount of empathy about our sister dying and shared with us the undeniable fact that Dad just wasn't the same. It made so much sense to us. We all were witnessing the same thing August III was and were hard-pressed to find an argument against what he was saying. We could see that our dad was declining and that he was depressed. His marriage was on the rocks. Additionally, August III had assured us our dad would have plenty to do. He made some good points. It made sense, but the way he went about ousting Dad still wasn't right.

I had no opportunity to "sock him in the puss." Adolphus started up the Jeep and we drove away. We didn't talk the entire way home. There was a deep sense of resignation that August III was now the head of Anheuser-Busch and there wasn't a damn thing we could do about it.

When we got back to Grant's Farm, Adolphus broke the news to Dad. I am not sure what was said or how he took it. I do know that Adolphus, at twenty-two years old, was far savvier than the rest of us. He had a better sense of what was going on in the company and what Dad was up against. He also knew he had to play his cards right. He had been groomed to take over the brewery someday too. With August III at the reins, his own position in the company would be tenuous. If he wanted to secure a leadership position at Anheuser-Busch or even lead the company himself someday, as he had hoped, he needed to stay in August III's good graces. It's not surprising he didn't push August III too much or defend my father too adamantly. He was looking out for himself.

The only ones who really had nothing to gain or lose were Andy and me. We were too young, and neither of us were in line to take over the company. We were living between two irrational people, so when we heard August III speak that day, it might have been the first rational thing we'd heard in years.

In the end, Dad would be able to run the farm, which was leased by the brewery, be the president of the Cardinals, and serve as honorary chairman of the board at Anheuser-Busch. Regardless, he was humiliated. He had a huge ego and hated being told what to do. He was approached by R. J. Reynolds and thought of partnering with them to retake control of Anheuser-Busch. One night, he woke Adolphus up and said, "I don't know what to do. This bastard son of mine has taken away my birthright." My father was torn. He had controlling stock in the company. He still had the ability to sell it if he wanted to. He was offered a handsome sum from R. J. Reynolds. But through tears, he told Adolphus, "But, son, I've thought about it. I just can't do it. I can't do that to my own father. I can't sell my family's company. I look at all that the company has been through. I look at what my grandfather, father, brother, and I have done . . . how much we cared for the company and the history and all that we took it through. I just can't sell. I just can't. I just can't do it." In the end, even though my father was devastated by what his own son had done to him, his loyalty to his father and grandfather's legacy superseded all. He couldn't let his company be led by anyone but a Busch. Family reigns after all. As heartbroken and disappointed as he was, he stepped down.

In a letter to his shareholders, he wrote:

I am writing each of you because I want to tell you as personally as I can, and with all the sincerity, how much I have deeply appreciated working with all of you through these years, no matter what the circumstances, no matter what the conditions, through Depressions and great wars through which our company has passed, no person could have received greater support or greater cooperation from those who own the company. As shareholders, those who have invested in this great company, we could not have become the leaders in the brewing industry and in the yeast business for so many years without your confidence and your support. So, through many years, through many letters, comments, and suggestions over the years, you have indicated your interest in Anheuser-Busch. I sincerely wish I could shake hands with each of the thousands of you and tell you how I feel. But since this is not possible, I am doing the next best thing, telling you, and what I wish I could tell you personally, as I pass the reins of the great company onto our executives, I promise you that as chairman of the board, I'll devote my time and energy to the continued success of Anheuser-Busch. I am sure the president and executives will carry on this tradition of those who founded this company and established the very high standards and principles which have guided me as the chief executive officer all these years. The heritage, which my father and my grandfather have left me, is the greatest contribution I can pass on. We have built an outstanding and competent management team. I know they will

accept again the challenges of the future and will
make this an even greater company upon my retirement
as CEO, chief executive officer. Several news stories
and articles have appeared in the St. Louis news media,
which I am taking the liberty of enclosing. The reason
I do this is so you will know whatever compliments are
paid to me, actually belong to you as stockholders.
Thank you again for your support. I wish each of you
a long life, good health, and prosperity.

                         With every good wish,
                         August Busch Jr.

What I find the most striking about this letter is the absence of
his son's name. He refused to call out August III by name as the future
leader of Anheuser-Busch. My dad was still filled with so much hatred
and rage toward August III and my sisters Lotsie and Elizabeth for their
lack of support of him. He felt most betrayed by Lotsie—who had at
one time helped him run the company and lived with him during his
divorce from Elizabeth, his second wife. None of us children were allowed to talk to any of them. There were no more Christmases, Easters,
Thanksgivings, or parties shared together.

While everything was falling apart around me, I found solace in the
farm. That remained steadfast. It always welcomed me hopefully at the
end of the day. Even if everything inside the Big House was changing,
I still had my friends on the farm and all the animals.

My father had made it out of that awful year. For twenty-eight years,
my dad ran the family empire. His accomplishments were many—including building nine breweries throughout the United States. He opened
theme parks, purchased the St. Louis Cardinals, brought St. Louis two
World Series wins, changed baseball by paying a player the first $100,000
salary, opened Grant's Farm to the public, and took Anheuser-Busch
out of Prohibition to be the number one beer company in the world.
He also transformed it from a three-million-barrel-a-year company to
a thirty-five-million-a-year one. He was a great philanthropist, and St.

Louis benefited enormously from this, especially St. Louis University and Washington University. By handing over distributorships, he made many people millionaires. He handed his son one of the most successful business stories and legacies the world had ever seen. He always said he had three loves in his life—his family, Anheuser-Busch, and St. Louis. And that was so true.

He should have been happy. He should have been excited to start enjoying his retirement. He was seventy-six and still had children at home. He should have been able to enjoy some peace. He deserved that.

But life had other plans.

Chapter Nine
NOT SO GLORY DAYS

By mid-1975, my mom started to spend about half of the year in Switzerland. My parents could barely stand the sight of each other. We kids didn't have much choice in the matter and just kept living our lives the same way we always had—according to the seasons. One big difference, though, was that my dad's personal secretary, Margaret Snyder, began to become a fixture in the house. Unfortunately, she was a hard pill to swallow and did her best to divide us from our dad. She seemed to make it her mission to capture all of Dad's attention so that he couldn't speak to any of us anymore. She was always beside him. I suppose she felt the need to protect him, considering what had happened with August III. I think she suspected all of us and saw us kids as potential threats to Dad in some way. To this day, I don't know what her deal was. I am not sure if it was insecurity on her part, or if my father directly asked her to look out for him, or both. I knew my father relied on her for everything now that my mother was gone so much, but it didn't make her presence any less annoying.

My sister Trudy actually sent a letter to my mom in Switzerland, where she was staying with my grandmother and most likely a boyfriend, begging her to come home at one point. She wrote that while she understood why she had to go, she missed her and asked why she wanted to stay away for so long. She also wrote about Margaret always being around, how she made Dad feel secure by acting like a mother toward him, showing she cared about him, telling him what to do, and answering questions for him before he could reply. But despite all that Margaret did, Trudy said he really needed and loved our mom more than anyone.

Another change was that we no longer talked to any of our half sisters. Though Lilly had been coming by once in a while immediately after Dad lost his position at the company, their relationship became strained. Ironically, it was because she, too, was still despondent and suffering from the loss of a child (her daughter Christy had died at twenty-two in 1969 from a cardiac incident, five years before my sister Christina) and also had been going through a divorce. You would think that my father might have had some compassion for his own child going through what he was going through, but he didn't. After being someone who was the life of the party, she declined rapidly upon her daughter's death. And it only got worse when her husband left her. To add insult to injury, she was now losing her dad to his own tragedy, and he was emotionally cold to her. (The reality was that he was cold to all of his children, not just her.) She took it personally though, and she attempted suicide by shooting herself in the head. She survived the attempt. By the time she was in her midfifties, she was bound to a wheelchair and was never the same until her death in 1995. Our father showed even less compassion toward her after the suicide attempt. Even though his father took his own life, he showed no sign of understanding what Lilly might be going through. He thought she was "nuts" to attempt suicide. He had no patience for her. It's as if he was the only one who was allowed to be in any sort of pain at all.

We weren't only having difficulties with our half siblings. There had been sibling rivalry among us seven kids for years, some of us more than others. Adolphus and Peter, the two oldest boys, went at it a lot. They were both extremely competitive, especially as teenagers. Maybe it was because we didn't have much supervision and, for the most part, were left to our own devices. Or maybe it was because we were never really taught positive conflict resolution. It's not like our parents set a great example. One day when Adolphus and Peter were both in high school, things escalated to the point that they decided to settle their argument in a duel out in the main hallway of the second floor. Our family was always a big gun family. We all collected guns of all kinds, including machine guns. My mom and dad were able to get any kind of gun available and often gifted them to us kids at Christmas, birthdays, and special occasions. Peter and Adolphus were especially into collecting and were enamored with guns. Each of them grabbed his machine gun from his room (one had an M1, the other an M16).

Andy and I were watching television in the Blue Room right off the end of the hallway and ran to stand in the doorway so we could watch it all go down.

My brothers stood at opposite ends of the hall with their guns pointed at one another. Yolanda stepped out into the hall and started screaming, "Boys, stop it! Put those guns down!"

Neither seemed willing to put his gun down.

Yolanda kept screaming, "You're not going to shoot each other!" And then she stepped between them, throwing herself in harm's way. While I can't say this with 100 percent certainty, I have reason to believe that both of their guns were loaded, and all that one of them had to do was pull the trigger and she would have most certainly been killed.

I stood there with my mouth open in utter disbelief, thinking over and over to myself, *This is crazy!*

It *was* crazy. Andy and I, who were only about twelve and eight years old at the time, were also in harm's way. I remember foolishly thinking that as long as I stood behind the threshold of the door, I would be safe should the bullets begin to spray into the room. It's astonishing really. Yolanda saved all of our lives that day.

It's not that my father didn't teach us gun safety. We all went shooting with my dad, and he taught us how to use a gun. Of course, he taught us that we should never point them at each other. But like all instructions to kids, they bear reminding. It was common for Peter and Adolphus to keep guns in their rooms, even after the duel incident. My brother Peter was never far from a gun, especially with all the talk of Patty Hearst's kidnapping. He was concerned and felt he needed protection. He even carried a .45 in an old Western-style holster. One day he shot himself in the leg. He accidentally pulled the trigger while practicing a quick draw from his holster. When all was said and done, he was fine, so my mom and dad didn't punish him. I suppose they thought he'd learned his lesson the hard way, and that real-life consequences were always the best teacher. The trouble was, for Peter, this was rarely the case.

One night, when Peter was twenty years old, his friend David Leeker was spending the night in his room. By then, Peter slept in a different wing of the house than I did, so I didn't know that David was even in the house.

When I woke up the next morning, Yolanda told me, "Billy, there has been an accident." My stomach dropped, thinking that something horrible like what happened to Christina and Andy had happened to another family member. I prepared myself to hear the worst. But it was even worse than I had imagined.

Yolanda said, "Peter shot and killed his friend David last night."

I stood there shocked and mute, as I had with the news about Nathan and Christina, having nothing to say. If I had questions or wondered anything about what had gone down, I didn't think to ask in that moment. There was no time for follow-up questioning anyway. Yolanda was adamant that I was to go to school that morning and never say a word to anyone about it.

As an adult now, I wonder if she was immediately briefed by my father's lawyers and instructed to tell us to go to school as usual and continue living as "normally" as possible—whatever normal was anymore.

I went to school that day, and one of the teachers came up to me and asked, quite concerned, "Billy, are you going to be okay? We heard what happened."

All I could say was, "I'm fine."

But the truth of it was, I wasn't. I felt terrible for Peter and for the Leeker family. It was horrific. But there was no one to talk to about it even if I wanted to. My mother was gone. I can't remember if we were instructed not to talk to Peter or if, once again, as with Andy, I couldn't muster the words to console him or ask him how he was doing. My father didn't seem to be too affected. I know he was in the house that night. I heard later that he was there when the ambulance came. I know that the room and carpet had been covered with blood and several farm-hands were called in to clean it up.

The police deemed the entire situation another accident, which it was. By then, Peter had a reputation for accidentally discharging fire-arms. No charges were ever filed against him. In an article the *New York Times* published the following day, they explained the incident.

As Peter and David prepared for bed, Peter went to get a pillow and returned with the pillow and a .357 Magnum Colt revolver. When Peter was putting the revolver away, it discharged as he threw the pillow to David. The bullet struck David in the face, sending him to St. Antho-ny's Hospital, where he was pronounced dead on arrival, only twenty minutes after the incident occurred.

When I say nothing happened, nothing happened. My father never spoke of the incident again; neither did Peter. Peter was clearly despon-dent. But none of us addressed the reason why. We all just went to school, but it was clear we needed our mother's help throughout this difficult time.

By the fall of that year, everything had escalated. In a letter to my mother—whom he called Trudy, short for Gertrude—my father relayed that he'd even kept things from her. (She was not happy at all about it.) He wrote:

September 30, 1976

Dearest Trudy,

I was happy to receive your letters and to know you are having a quiet, wonderful time. I hope Mami's broken toe is not too painful.

I've thought about what you said in your letters. Most of my business interests these days involves baseball. Yet when I tried to discuss the problems, you hung up the phone several times. You also changed the subject in the middle of the conversation. So in my book, there's nothing to tell. As far as Peter is concerned, there was only one problem I did not discuss with you ONLY because all attorneys made me promise not to tell anyone. They had good and valid reasons for doing so and that situation still holds.

I realize I get loud and short-tempered at times. But I resent constantly being downed and belittled in front of the children, friends, and servants. After all, I am the father and head of the house! Yet, at times, it appears the servants are treated with more consideration and respect than I.

You know, too, how I want the pictures, art, objects, and furniture at Grant's Farm to remain in place. Things are constantly being moved around, and when I ask about them, I can never get a satisfactory answer. You must know, after all these years, what that does to me.

Since you were open and frank with me, I hope you will accept my comments in the same spirit. Perhaps it is healthy to exchange these thoughts by letter, because we can't seem to do so in person.

The weather is delightful, but we still have no rain, just a few showers. We're pumping out the lakes to provide all possible water for the trees, in an effort to save them.

The children are fine . . . busy with school and homework.

We miss you and send much love to you and Mami + A BIG KISS.

Yours,

Gussie

The letter was typed, and no doubt Margaret typed all of my father's correspondences. I noticed "+ a big kiss" was added in his own handwriting when he sent it. It was clear that he and my mom were arguing over phone calls—about everything from the business (the Cardinals) to Peter's accident and the household items. I know my father still loved her, but things were getting increasingly contentious—even when my mother wasn't physically living in the house.

Then one day, when I was about eighteen, all of us kids were called into the gun room. My dad was sitting in there, and Adolphus was standing right behind him, acting as his lawyer or enforcer. Without much of an introduction or setup to soften the blow, my dad looked at us and said, "Your mom and I are getting a divorce. We're going to let her stay in the cottage when she comes back from Switzerland until we get her her own house. But she no longer is allowed at the Big House."

He looked sad and depressed. He told us in a very matter-of-fact way that she'd been having an affair and he couldn't take it any longer, that it was over. Up until then, I didn't know for sure that Mom was having an affair. I think I might have heard that she'd cheated on him. There was a rumor that she went upstairs and had sex with somebody at one of the parties that they'd thrown at the house. But this news struck me.

By the time I heard my father say the word *divorce*, it all felt a bit anticlimactic, something of an inevitability. Mom wasn't around much anyway, and when she was, she and my dad were fighting all the time. Knowing about the affair, it made sense why my dad would want a divorce. It wasn't the worst thing that could happen to us. We had all lived through so much worse by then; it felt like a minor tragedy in comparison to what happened to Christina, Nathan, and David Leeker. In fact, a divorce felt like a relief in many ways. Finally, things could quiet down and be normal. We all knew, deep down, that my mother wasn't the only one having an affair—or who'd had affairs. Back then (and I am not saying it's right) it was expected that a man could have affairs, but a woman could not. It was just the way it was. My mother was supposed to tolerate my father's infidelities throughout their marriage, but my father had no capacity to endure my mother's.

Eventually, my mother did return and stayed at the cottage. We kids would go there to see her and have dinner, until a house was bought for her in an area of town called Town and Country. We all thought she would fight for custody of us, but she didn't. There seemed to be no point since I was eighteen years old and Andy was happy living at Grant's Farm. In the end, she did exactly what she was told. She didn't try to visit the Big House, even though Dad was worried that she was going to go in and take things out.

It was a lonely and sad time. The glory days of living on Grant's Farm were now nothing more than a sweet memory. Margaret, now a permanent fixture, kept a close eye on Dad. It was strange and perturbing. Margaret and his lawyer, Mr. Susman, were really controlling him and making it impossible for us kids to have any kind of relationship with him. The house was an empty shell, just like my father. He walked around the house depressed and unhappy. His health also seemed to be waning.

I threw myself into football and trying to get the hell out of there. I got offers to play for a few small colleges, but I chose to go to Mizzou—the Columbia campus of the University of Missouri, the school I'd always dreamed of playing for and going to. The university told my dad that they were going to give me a scholarship, but my dad said, "No, you don't have to give him a scholarship. We've got the money to pay the tuition. Give it to somebody who needs it."

The divorce was finalized in 1978, just in time for me to leave for college. On the day in August when I had to head out of town for football training camp, my dad was looking so old and run-down. He was still smoking heavily and suffering through bouts of pneumonia. I loaded up my truck and said goodbye to all the staff. Then I climbed the stairs to my father's bedroom. When I got to the door of his room, he was lying in his bed with all the curtains closed, blocking out most of the light. It was late that morning, almost noon, and he wasn't out of bed. Seeing him lie there was such a stark contrast to the active, bustling father I recalled from my childhood.

Something caught in my throat at the sight of him. He looked for sure like he might die.

"Hey, Dad," I called out. "I'm leaving."

He looked over and seemed stunned to see me there. "Where are you going?" he asked.

"I'm going to college. I'm on the football team. I have to get there early."

He stared at me for a beat, and I felt the bulge in my throat rise as I fought back tears. "Jesus Christ, pal, I am so proud of you." And then he started to cry.

I bent over and kissed him and told him I loved him, even though he couldn't quite muster those words for me.

I turned around and walked out as fast as I could, and as soon as I was out of his sight, I ran down the hall and the stairs, out the door, and straight to our family chapel, where I fell to my knees. I had to get away from everyone—the house was already bustling with staff members and kitchen workers—and I didn't want to be seen.

For the first time in my life, the tears finally came. They came for Christina, for Nathan, for Andy, for Peter, for David, for my mother and father's marriage, for all the memories of happier times that were now only a distant memory, and most of all, for my dad. I cried at what he had become—what we had all become. I cried for what we all once had and lost. I cried because, in my heart of hearts, I thought for certain that that kiss goodbye was the last goodbye, and that I would never see my father alive again. I did not think he could survive this final heartbreak.

When the last tear fell, I wiped it. I stood up, walked back to the Big House, jumped in my truck, and hightailed it out of there. Just as my grandfather had wanted to "go West, young man" so long ago and separate himself as far as he could from his father's legacy to make his own way, I followed, heading that way too. It was Mizzou, so it wasn't quite the Wild West, but in so many ways it was the beginning of some wild times. And I was ready for them.

Anyplace else was a better place to be.

Chapter Ten
WILD, WILD WEST

As soon as I arrived on campus, I threw myself into playing football. I was so proud to be playing for the University of Missouri. What a team we had in 1978. The highlights were shutting out Notre Dame at their home field with Joe Montana as their quarterback, beating Nebraska at Husker Stadium, and finishing the season by winning the Liberty Bowl over a strong LSU team in Memphis. It was just a wonderful experience all around. I was strong and healthy; being far away from home suited me. I felt like I was heading in a good direction, and for the first time, I had a sense of what I wanted to do with my life. Even though I was taking courses in nutrition, agriculture, and business (a mixture of all the subjects I loved), all I really wanted to do was play football. When I wasn't in class or on the field, I was living in a dorm room with my best friend from St. Louis. Everything just felt easygoing and relaxed. I was no longer coming home to an awkward or stressful situation every day. By the time I left Grant's Farm, I was totally convinced that my father was going to die. But word came from back home that he was rallying. I also heard that he and his secretary, Margaret, were an official item.

It was truly the perfect time to be away. I felt more at home at college than I did in my own home. That's what I loved and appreciated most about Mizzou. I wasn't ever lonely. Even though I wasn't in an official fraternity, being a part of the football team made me feel like I was. I had so many friends, I could hardly keep up. I lived for the weekend—the games and the parties that followed (and thanks to the movie *Animal House*, wild toga keggers were all the rage). All these years later, I can still feel the exhilaration of Saturday afternoons and running out of the tunnel to hear the roar of seventy thousand people cheering us on. It made my hair stand on end every time, and just thinking about it today makes it do the same. At night there was ample beer and beautiful college girls. I didn't have a care in the world. It was the kind of start to a college career every boy dreams about, but it wasn't a dream. I was living it. It didn't even register that my parents weren't there in the stands on game day. Dad was off with Margaret now, and Mom had her Italian boyfriend keeping her busy. Still, I felt like Grant's Farm had prepared me well for life on a college campus. In many ways, the "bubble" that was college was similar to the one I'd lived in on Grant's Farm. I felt protected and special in both places.

As a football player, I enjoyed the celebrity status that came with wearing a Mizzou uniform. For the first time in my life, I felt like this was something that I did all by myself, without riding the coattails of my father. He didn't even have an interest in football. This was all me. But some aspects of living on the farm I took with me. Just like at home, I made friends like it was my business. I became friendly with all the coaches and all the hardworking people on campus. I had been raised to understand that I wasn't better than anyone just because we had more money than most people. Even though the Busch name meant something to every Missourian, it didn't change the way I behaved. I was taught to respect everyone. Nevertheless, I was still very much shielded from the hard truths of the real world as a football player on campus.

Of course, when I wasn't playing games or when we had a holiday, I went home—mostly to duck hunt and visit the farm. Grant's Farm was only about two hours from Mizzou, even if it felt like a million miles. Andy was playing high school football now, and I enjoyed going to see him play. Like most kids, I went home for the summer and worked on the farms (both Grant's and Belleau) and played as much polo as I could. Adolphus, Andy, and I played together, and we won the Inter-Circuit Cup, which qualified us for Nationals that September. I was supposed to be back at Mizzou in August for football training; however, Adolphus was adamant. He said, "Come on, you're going to get hurt playing football. Let's go to Nationals."

I was torn between my love of football and college and playing polo. But in the end, my brother's persuasion was hard to resist. Reluctantly, I agreed to move back home. I called Warren Powers, who was the head coach at Mizzou at the time, and told him that I wasn't going to be returning. I was raised to honor my responsibilities and let people know personally when I couldn't do so. He was as nice as could be.

"Thank you for your time," he said. "We had great hopes for you and really appreciated having you on our team."

It was a difficult phone call for me. I knew I wasn't the star of the team, but the coaches made me feel like a big part of it. I also knew the coaches would be disappointed. Thankfully for me, Coach Powers made it easy.

In the fall of 1979, I enrolled at the University of Missouri–St. Louis (UMSL), thirty minutes from Grant's Farm, and went straight into training for polo Nationals. Within a matter of months, my entire life spiraled. During a practice match, I broke my arm. So much for Adolphus's comment that I would get hurt in football and not polo. The irony! My cousin had to sub in and play in Nationals on my behalf.

Being unable to compete in either polo or football was painful. To add insult to injury, college was different at UMSL. Without the football team, it wasn't as much fun. In fact, I hated it. I went from feeling like I had my whole life figured out to suddenly not having any idea what I wanted to do. I hated living at home at Grant's Farm too. Margaret was there all the time. Over the next two years, she took control of everything and continued to do her best to separate Dad from us kids. In many ways, I felt like I was losing the Grant's Farm I'd grown up on. While living at Mizzou, I'd felt like I belonged everywhere, but now I felt like I didn't belong anywhere. I felt like a stranger in my own home.

My father secretly married Margaret in 1981. She was now, indeed, what she had hoped to become all along: the new "queen of the castle." And she wanted nothing to do with the former queen's children.

At one point, Margaret thought it would be a great idea if she and my father bought themselves a home in Arizona. They shipped all the horses—even the driving horses and mules—out there. Margaret thought the dry Arizona air would be better for Dad's health. The night before they left, I overheard her talking to Joseph, the butler. She said to him, "Now you watch these kids, and you make sure they don't do anything to or take anything from this house! Make sure nothing is destroyed. If they let anything happen to this house and this farm, you call us right away! We'll take care of the situation!"

Joseph, to my shock, replied, "Yes, ma'am. Yes, Mrs. Busch, yes. I will make sure I will watch them very, very closely."

I was disgusted with Joseph for believing that we would disrespect Grant's Farm in any way. We loved our home. There was no way we would ever abuse it. What was also shocking about Joseph's response was that he was always so faithful to us (when he wasn't beating us up) and to my mother, but now how quickly his loyalties had turned. And he wasn't the only one. There were other employees and friends who sucked up to Margaret now that she was married to Dad. That's what was so damned sickening with these people and Margaret. How could they think we were out to get our own father? We were the ones who had his back for years. We were the ones who took care of the farm. We would have protected it and him with everything we had.

I can see now that she and all the others were insecure. They were also taking advantage of my father themselves. It was a classic case of projection. Every accusation Margaret was making was really a confession of her own behavior and motives. It was a huge lesson in life for me. As a child, of course I saw how power shifted when my father lost the company. But this was the first time as an adult that I observed the *loyalty* shift. And since then, loyalty has been something I value in life, because I saw how quickly people who said they were your "friends" and even "family" turned their back as soon as someone else had more power or authority. It stuck with me then and sticks with me today. There were exceptions: Frank, Rollins, and Warren. Their loyalty never wavered, and they were as disgusted as I was with the way things had become.

It was clear to me, to all of my siblings, that my father, in his late age and fragile state, was being completely brainwashed and taken advantage of by Margaret. He listened to everything she said, without question. I remember one time when she made him literally turn his back on his favorite niece, Sally Wheeler, his brother's daughter. They had been close friends and were in the horse business together. He truly loved Sally, and Sally revered my father as her own after her father passed. Margaret couldn't handle my father having affection for anyone but her. Dad clearly wanted to talk to Sally, but Margaret wouldn't allow it. I wrote a letter to Sally and explained to her that it was not Dad but Margaret who had caused the division and that we loved her and missed seeing her.

Margaret treated us six kids from my mother, Trudy, the same way. She felt differently about the other children, especially August III, whom she favored. She frequently brought August III to the house and did her darndest to kowtow to the guy who now had the power. She would fall all over herself, gushing over August whenever he would fly his helicopter in and land it right outside our house.

To say I was confused, bitter, and angry would be an understatement. Here was my father and his new wife greeting, hugging, and humoring the man whom he'd taught us all to hate. What happened to "Sock 'em in the puss, Billy"? We weren't supposed to talk to August III, or any of our other siblings who took his side, ever again. Our family was torn apart when August III decided to take over the company, and now my father and his new wife were suddenly enamored with him.

I'd ask, "What the hell is going on?" And as usual, there was never an explanation. No one ever talked to us. To me, it was like watching an absurd comedy. Suddenly, my dad, who was at death's door before I left for college, had a new lease on life. Margaret started inviting all sorts of unsavory characters and hangers-on to the house whose only mission was to milk Dad for everything he had. I had to laugh—Margaret had convinced him he had to watch out for us, his own children, who loved and defended him, while she invited veritable pariahs into his life. She completely blocked his loved ones' access but allowed grifters in without batting an eyelash.

In the spring of 1981, Dad and Margaret traveled to Florida for spring training and, I suppose, a honeymoon. We had something we wanted to tell him about Grant's Farm and were unable to get ahold of him. We tried and tried to call him, but Margaret refused to let our dad talk to us. Finally, I took the phone, dialed it, and pretended to be the baseball player, Garry Templeton.

I said, "Yes, ma'am, this is Garry Templeton. I need to speak to Mr. Busch."

Immediately, the phone was handed over to Dad.

"Dad, it's me, Billy!" I said quickly. He seemed surprised and happy to hear from me. I laugh about it now, but I remember being so disappointed. The only way I was able to get through to my father was by pretending to be a baseball player.

I felt so unmoored and unhappy during this time. I hated school, and I wasn't doing well. I was flunking everything because I wouldn't go to class. I hung out in the rec room on campus and played games or slept on a couch all morning. In the afternoon, I would head back home to work. The only part of my life where I felt at ease was when I was working on Grant's Farm with the crew and the animals. It kept me grounded enough not to go crazy, and I do think that could've been a possibility. When my work at the farm was done, I'd head out and party. I rarely came home to sleep. Instead, I'd crash wherever I could.

I was still working out and was strong as a bull, thanks to my days on the farm. I just didn't know how strong I was until one fateful January night. I was hanging out at one of my favorite bars in a kind of redneck part of town. My friend, the bouncer of the bar, and I were there late, closing the place down. There were some guys we didn't know there too. The next thing I knew, some big guy wanted to arm-wrestle me. I've never been one to turn down a competition. We started to arm-wrestle, and I won. Since he was a big guy, he was genuinely shocked and accused me of cheating.

"Let's do it again!" he said.

We went again. I beat him handily. His buddies then started to yell at him, and they wanted to fight me.

The only reason I went outside with all of them was because the bouncer, my friend, was a tough guy, and I knew he'd have my back if the guy's buddies jumped me. He was so big and tough, in fact, that I knew he could take the whole lot of them if I needed him to. And I felt confident that if the guy threw a punch, I had a good chance of beating him.

It must have been below zero that night. The buddies all formed a circle around us, blocking me and their friend in. The guy threw the first punch, and we started to fight. It was clear it wasn't going to be easy. We were both slipping all over a sheet of ice. We finally got on the ground, and I pinned his arms behind him. He was going nuts trying to get loose, and all of a sudden, I heard his buddies chanting: "Bite him! Bite him!" And sure enough, the bastard tried to bite me on the neck. I got him pinned, and he tried again.

"That's enough," I told him, "you're done!"

But he had this fire in his eyes. His mouth opened and he tried to bite me again.

I started yelling, "You son of a bitch! What the hell!"

And that's when I bent down and bit him back. I bit right into his ear. He yanked his head away from me, and when I came up, I had his ear in my mouth. It was the most unbelievable thing. He was still so crazy and trying to fight that he didn't realize his ear had come off!

And when I say his ear came off, I mean *his ear came off*—as if it had been surgically removed. The whole ear was ripped off the side of his head. I mean, I've seen some weird shit in my day, but that was the weirdest.

His friends started shouting, "Your ear is gone! Your ear is gone!"

That's when he stopped. Everybody was in shock. Somebody had enough sense to take his ear and put it in a cup filled with snow and tell the guy that he needed to go to the hospital. The guy left, and there was nothing for me to do but go back to the bar. Obviously.

It was past closing time, and the only people left were the owner and my bouncer friend. We were sitting there, incredulous about what just happened. We kept saying, "I can't believe that just happened."

The next morning, of course, I got a call that my dad and his lawyer, Mr. Susman, wanted to speak to me.

I showed up and my dad called me into his room.

"Jesus Christ, what the hell did you do last night?"

I didn't know what to say.

"Did you bite somebody's ear off?"

"Yeah, Dad, I did."

"Jesus Christ."

My dad was just disgusted. I was disgusted too—I certainly wasn't proud. I was still seriously confused and shocked by what had happened. It was all over the news—on the television, in the newspaper, on the radio. They were painting me as a pretty horrible person. All the PR people at Anheuser-Busch were involved by now and were looking for ways to contain the mess. They were very worried about how it was going to affect the company. And I bet August III felt self-righteous and vindicated (and a bit superior) now. He didn't say it outright, but we all felt that he wanted to say, "See! I told you so! This is why we don't bring my half siblings into the company!" It wasn't good luck for the company, for the family, or for me, who was trashed in the press at every turn.

"We're going to have to pay 'em off," Susman piped in. "You've maimed somebody."

"What do you mean?" I asked. "That guy was the one who started the fight! He took the first swing! He challenged me first! We started the fight, and then he tried to bite me! So I bit him back. Why would we have to pay him? He had it coming to him!"

"Your name is B-U-S-C-H. It doesn't matter whether or not you started it. If you've got the money, you've got to pay."

It was my first real-life adult experience outside the bubble, and it wasn't pretty. It was awful. My father was disappointed and angry. I was disappointed and angry. I also felt the injustice of it all. I didn't ask to fight this guy. He was the one looking for a fight. But I learned a valuable lesson that night. If you play, you have to pay. It's how the world works, even more so with a name like Busch.

The good news was I didn't have to go to jail for it. For that I am grateful. As far as I know, that guy got his money.

Ironically, despite what happened, the owner of the bar asked me if I wanted to be his partner. I had gotten to know him when I was a regular customer, and he pointed out that I was already there all the time. So I ended up getting into the bar business, buying a 50 percent share of the place and dropping out of school to work there full-time.

This was where my true education began. For the first time in my life, I was learning what it meant to be in business. I was learning how the world worked, but also how people worked. And it wasn't all pretty. Well, some of it was. And by *some*, I mean a girl named Christi.

Chapter Eleven
GOODBYE

Buying the bar and running it for three years was an education I couldn't get at any university. One of my first tasks was to clean up all the craziness that went on there. When I started running the place, it was basically a roadhouse—not the kind of bar you'd take your mom to. My friend, the bouncer who had my back in the fight, was a real Patrick Swayze–type of guy (only bigger) and helped me weed out the riffraff.

During those years, it was a wonder I didn't get killed by some of the patrons who frequented the place, like one guy who went by the name Biker Bob, a trained killer and mercenary. One night he came in looking for me and wanted to settle the score for the guy who had his ear bitten off. High on drugs and acting crazy, he came right up to me and asked, "Are you Billy Busch?"

I denied it (of course) and said, "I think I saw Billy just leave."

My fighting days were behind me. I tried hard to clean up my image, and the image of the bar. My father had always been opposed to people who couldn't handle alcohol. And, at the time, there were a lot of people who couldn't do that at my bar. I tried my best to figure out a way to deal with it. It wasn't easy. I made a lot of mistakes, and looking back, there are things I wish I'd done differently. I was naive when I started. I learned in a hurry the things you could get away with in the bar business that were unethical, and I didn't want any part of it. I knew my dad wouldn't have done business this way, and I didn't want to either.

It was there that I learned what life was like outside the bubble of Grant's Farm. I learned pretty quickly that people were out to get something from me and expected a lot from me because of my name. I had to become very cautious of whom I called a "friend." Everyone always wanted me around when it was time to pay the bill or when they wanted baseball tickets and the like, but after the game was over, I'd never hear from them again. I started to become a bit suspicious of men—and women. I became more realistic. I learned that not everybody out in the world is going to be sincere.

As an adult, I started to see the varnish fade on the shiny veneer that was the Busch Family Fairy Tale. I had always been a bit naive and bought into the fairy tale hook, line, and sinker. My sister Trudy would even often say to me, "Billy, we are living in a fairy tale. We have a fairy-tale life." But that was only half true. Two truths can exist at the same time, which makes reality all the harder to comprehend and dissect as the years go by. Yes, we had fairy-tale parties, experiences, and money, and yes, people used us, our parents neglected us, and we grew up not knowing how to trust other people or how to love each other.

The more I got out into the real world and saw how others behaved, the more aware I became of my own cognitive dissonance. On the one hand, I loved my mom, dad, and family members, and on the other hand, I could see they weren't the best role models of human virtue. Nothing was ever consistent either. There were times I look back on and think, *Man, did that actually happen?* Yes, my mom threw lavish parties and knew how to celebrate a holiday, but she also lined my brothers and sisters up and whipped them in front of their friends and our employees for throwing outdoor furniture cushions in the pool to use as flotation devices. As kids, we never knew what to expect from our parents, and as we grew, I think a lot of us kids internalized all this trauma and behavior, and instead of doing something about it and getting the help we needed, we acted out in a lot of the same ways. We snapped at and turned on each other, just as our mother and father had turned on us.

But despite it all, I was hell-bent on trying to pretend everything had indeed been that fairy tale because, quite honestly, it was easier and less painful than dealing with the truth of it all. And the truth was, I never knew if I was coming or going with any of them. I never had a sibling who had my back unconditionally. My father had always warned us that the largest number of friends we could really count on would be two or three. And for a brief time, I thought those "friends" were my three brothers.

For a few years in the 1980s, Adolphus, Peter, Andy, and I, the four horsemen as depicted by the Remington bronze, got the Busch company to sponsor our polo team, and we played competitively all over the country. During those years, we were probably the closest we had ever been—and ever would be. After I sold the bar in 1983, Adolphus, Andy, and I purchased an Anheuser-Busch distributorship in Homestead, Florida. Since August III had to approve owners of distributorships, he had to grant us permission to do so as well. Ultimately, he allowed us to have it because if we were preoccupied with a distributorship, we wouldn't make waves or try to work for the company itself. In many ways, he knew we didn't pose a threat of any kind by owning a distributorship. And it turned out to be a great business for a little while.

We were closer during those years not only because of polo and the distributorship, but also because of what was happening back at Grant's Farm. We all knew Margaret had turned our father on us. She was doing her best to keep our dad from us, and there was a real possibility that she would also try to dissuade our dad from leaving us Grant's Farm in his will. The only thing we kids had, and truly loved, was the farm. August III had the company and was running it, and we were never going to be able to touch that. I loved the farm more than anything. It was the best part of my childhood, and all the animals on the farm were my friends. Moreover, I considered many of those that worked on the farm my dearest friends and family. The idea that Margaret might somehow come in during the final years of Dad's life and persuade him to write all his kids off, bonded us together in a way we had never been before.

By 1986 I had already decided it was time to finish my degree at St. Louis University; I started taking classes again and working alongside Andy at Grant's Farm. We had gone to an animal sale in Macon, Missouri, and there we saw a baby African elephant, two years old, go up for auction. We immediately called our dad, and even in his old age, he knew a good thing when he heard it. "Buy the goddamned thing," he said. Andy and I were so excited. It had been years since Grant's Farm had an elephant. We had stopped hauling elephants from Busch Gardens in Tampa, to St. Louis several years before, and, like her namesake, my Tessie had been sold to the Ringling Brothers circus. They knew great elephants when they saw them.

Since we had the new baby elephant, we knew we needed to get a companion for it. So, we bought another one, a female. We named the pair Bud and Mickey (after Budweiser and Michelob, naturally) and brought them back to Grant's Farm. While I was going to school, my project was to train the elephants. I had so much fun with them. Dad loved them too, especially when I would bring the elephants right inside the Big House, where he was, to brighten his spirits. He'd sit there and feed them peanuts, fruits, and vegetables and pet them. Sometimes, when Dad was sitting on the porch, I would walk the elephants into the pond so he could watch them play, swim, trumpet, and blow water all over themselves. Dad got a huge kick out of that. I remembered the stories he used to tell me of the times he'd ride his horse up the stairs into his dad's bedroom to make him laugh. I couldn't help but think he was remembering those times, too, when I brought the elephants inside to see him. I was so grateful for those times. Seeing him smile and laugh in those final years was a rare gift.

In 1987 my brothers and I arrived home after spending the winter in Florida, where we'd been playing polo all season. I planned to attend school and work with the elephants again so they could perform in the elephant shows. When I made my way up from the Big House to see the elephants, I'd pass by not only the capuchin monkeys, who were performing tricks and collecting coins from the guests, but their beautiful trainer as well. One day, as I was walking by them, I thought to myself, *Who is this pretty girl?* Every day I would walk by her as I headed to the elephants. I'd try to say hello, but she wasn't interested. I couldn't tell if she was just shy or if she didn't like me. She'd put her head down and look away. But I was persistent. I found out her name from another guy who worked at Grant's Farm. Christi. She was the talk of the farm for all the men who worked there.

I ended up buying some more monkeys so I'd have an excuse to spend more time with her. I asked her if she would help me, and she flat out said, "No." When she finally did decide to help me with the monkeys, they loved her and hated me. Before long Christi had these two young monkeys on a leash, eating out of the palm of her hand. I realized that if she could train those wild monkeys, she could handle someone like me.

One day the monkeys were biting me, and out of frustration I snapped and asked Christi if she would finish up for the day and clean out their cages.

"I don't work for you," she said. "Clean your own cages." And she walked out.

After that, I was officially smitten. I did everything I could to make her talk to me again. I even asked her if I could drive her convertible.

"Yes," she said. "As long as you can take it up to the shop and air up the tires." What a turnaround—now I was working for her. I thought she was playing hard to get, but the truth of the matter was she was shy, only nineteen years old, and didn't quite know what to make of me. After I first visited her, the other workers began warning her about the reputation my family had. She could be setting herself up for trouble.

Finally, a big opportunity for a date came up. Margaret and Dad were throwing my brother August III a lavish fiftieth birthday party. So I asked Christi, "Do you want to come with me as my date?"

There were other people and workers all standing around, and she didn't know what to say. She didn't want to look like she was going out with the boss's son. She also didn't know what my story was, except for the rumors she'd heard.

I stood there for a while, waiting for her to make up her mind. "I got to know now. It's happening tonight."

At last, she said, "Yes," and then immediately asked, "What do I wear?"

"Oh, it's casual," I said. "Meet me back here in an hour and a half."

So off she went, and when she came back, she stepped out of her car in a little skirt and blazer. She looked around at the other women arriving in long gowns, pearls—the works—and said she wanted to turn around and leave. To this day she swears that if she'd had a cell phone back then, that's exactly what she would have done. She would have called me and said, "Nope. Not doing this." But because she didn't want to stand me up, she honored her word and went up to the house.

Our entire family was coming out when she was walking up to meet me, and the way she tells it, everyone looked at her and then at me as if to say, *My God, Billy, what did you just pick up? Where did you find this one?* I took one look at her and I thought she was absolutely beautiful. She didn't need a gown or fancy jewelry. I took her by the arm and together we walked to the Bauernhof, where the party was held.

As soon as we got to the party, she felt uncomfortable. For a time, she snuck off and hung out with her employee friends until she felt better. Eventually, she knew she had to come back to the table. She told me she felt entirely out of place, but I thought she was perfect. Later that night, I took her out on a golf cart, and we drove around the grounds and had so much fun. It was the first of what would become many dates.

The next two years were both thrilling and exhilarating. What I loved most about Christi was that she could take me or leave me. She had her own life. She wasn't possessive. She was far from impressed that I was a Busch. And she never, not for one second, bought into the idea that I lived a fairy-tale life. She was a hard worker, hustling at several different jobs while also working as a cosmetologist and putting herself through college. She was no gold digger and had zero patience or tolerance for people who put on airs or thought they were better than anyone else because of how much money they had or what their name was. She was also loyal and a fierce defender of me. I realized she was looking out for me when others, who said they were, weren't.

Interestingly, Margaret liked Christi. She could sense what I did—that Christi wasn't interested in "being a Busch." She was truly interested in me. She also loved that Christi went out of her way to take care of my dad. In the last two years of Dad's life, Christi was always there for him. Whenever she came over, Margaret would say, "Darling, your girlfriend is here." My dad would get this big twinkle in his eye, and as someone who always had a soft spot for beautiful women, he would light up. He'd give her his hand and a little file. He loved having his hands touched and rubbed. Christi would also sneak him cigarettes. She would sit and listen to him talk or play cards with him so Margaret could get a break. I would even leave the two of them and go out for beers with the guys. She was patient and kind, and my father adored her. "Wow, pal, she's good-lookin'. You better hold on to this one," he'd say to me.

In 1988, to the shock of all of us—well, quite frankly, it was a relief—Margaret died suddenly of a brain hemorrhage. It was a shock because she was seventeen years younger than my dad, and we all expected her to outlive him. It was a relief because we knew that without her around, there wouldn't be any further interference in our relationship with Dad. For one blessed year, we had him to ourselves. By then he was old and feeble, and we all needed to be looking out for him, especially now that Margaret wasn't there. And sure enough, it didn't take long for someone to come along and try to take advantage of him.

One night Frank, my dad's valet, came to me and said, "Billy, I just got to tell you—that night nurse and your daddy are talking about marriage."

I was incredulous. "What?"

"They're talking about getting married!"

I thought to myself, *Oh shit, we're not going through this again. Now the night nurse is after Dad for his money.* Dad was almost ninety years old, and this nurse was in her thirties. People do just want something for nothing in this life, and if they have the opportunity to take it, they will take it.

I knew she worked from 10:00 p.m. to 6:00 a.m., so early the next morning I waited in the kitchen for her to come down from my dad's room. When she did, I asked if we could talk for a second.

She said, "Yes?"

"I understand that you're talking to my dad about marriage. Let me just tell you that's unprofessional, and if I ever hear about this again, you won't be welcome back in this place. I better never hear another word about you marrying my dad. Do you understand?"

She got really embarrassed because she knew she'd been caught. She said, "Yes." And the next night she called in and told the nursing service that she wasn't coming back to Grant's Farm. And that was the last we saw of her.

We bought a house for my father down in South Florida so he could be closer to Andy, Adolphus, and Peter, who were still playing polo. I was running our recently acquired distributorship in Houston, and along with Christi, I would visit him in Florida often.

Dad brought his coach horses down with him that winter. He would go out on the coach every day with Frank still by his side. My brothers were all there too, and so was I, as much as possible. It was great to be able to spend one-on-one time with him. It was like we had our dad back again, after nearly a decade of being kept apart.

In the spring of 1989, he headed back to Grant's Farm and his health started to deteriorate. He was still driving the horses every day, but for the most part, he was declining, and we could tell he didn't have long. On September 29, 1989, surrounded by his children, my father died in the same bed where his father had taken his own life. When he took his last breath and the nurses pronounced him dead, we heard the elk bugle in the Deer Park, as if to cry out, *The King of Beers is dead*. All of Grant's Farm was in mourning—it seemed even the animals knew. August III, the family stoic who never showed emotion, broke down and started crying. *Our dad* was dead.

We loved him, and now he was gone. He wasn't the King of Beers to us. At the time of his death, Dad had repaired his relationships with his children. He and August III were friends again. We were all doing our best to get along. The only one who was not there when Dad died was Adolphus. He harbored so much bitterness toward August III that he couldn't stand to be in the same room with him.

Dad's funeral, which was held at the new Cathedral Basilica of St. Louis, wasn't so much a somber affair as a celebration of life. The massive church was packed. There was a huge public outpouring. People lined the road from Grant's Farm up to the cemetery. This was because he was a legend. He was someone we all respected. He did a lot in his lifetime for other people, for the business. He was leaving an enormous legacy, one that his forebears had left him, but he was leaving it even stronger and better than it was before. Here was a guy who lived life to the fullest in every way imaginable, and he was lucky enough to be able to live a long time. He lived until he was ninety. He had seen the turn of the century. He had lived through two world wars, a depression, and Prohibition, and had built an internationally known company. When he took over the company in 1946, it was producing just over three million barrels of beer, and when he left in 1974, the company was producing thirty-four million barrels.

We buried him at Sunset Cemetery alongside Margaret, his father, mother, brother, and of course, Christina.

Seeing him in the final year of his life, so sick and so weak, we all saw it as a huge relief that he was no longer in any pain or suffering. We all had a sense of happiness for the good life that he lived, loving his brewery, his farm, and his family.

Chapter Twelve
NEW RULES

One of the greatest joys of my life is knowing that my father met and loved Christi before he died. There was truly something special about her, and even my father could tell. Two years after my father's death, in 1991, I was in Florida again playing polo, and Christi came down to stay with me. At one point she said, "I've got to leave. I have to get back to work."

I pleaded with her, "I don't want you to go. What if I said I want to marry you? Then would you stay?"

She said yes.

It wasn't very romantic, but it was sincere. I didn't want to spend my life without her. She eventually asked me to get on one knee and to ask her father for her hand. I had never heard you were supposed to do these things—they were completely foreign concepts to me. In my mother's worldview, people should be getting on their knees to ask us Busches if they could be a part of our family. But Christi was so down-to-earth and reminded me every day what it was like in the real world. She kept me tethered to it.

Christi grew up in a middle-class blue-collar family near Grant's Farm. She would be the first to bristle if someone said her marriage to me was a "Cinderella story." She was no pauper by any standards, she'd argue. Her parents both worked hard, and she went to private Catholic schools. I respected her for the morals and values she possessed. She had a no-nonsense approach to life, and she was not one to tolerate disrespect or injustices to anyone.

Becoming a Busch was quite an experience for her—for both of us really. As much as my father loved and adored her, my mother wasn't her biggest fan. Truth be told, my mother wasn't a fan of anybody, including her own kids at times. My mother was difficult. It wasn't until I had entered the real world and the blinders came off that I could see it. In this new light, my mother wasn't just a *regal*, noble queen. She was also judgmental and harsh. She was like a "queen on steroids," as Christi would say. She had a habit of playing us siblings against each other.

Christi's first meeting with her was less than ideal. My mother was visiting Adolphus at Belleau Farm, and on the way there I told Christi that she doesn't like long hair or painted fingernails. Of course, Christi had long blond hair and brightly painted fingernails.

"Oh, she's going to hate me. Why are we going to see her?"

My siblings weren't exactly welcoming to Christi either. When we got there, my mom and my sisters, Trudy and Beaty, thought it would be a fun sport to order around Adolphus's wife while she served them. They would laugh and say, "The champagne isn't cold enough. Go get us some cold champagne."

"Oh, we love to make them cry," we heard one of them say after seeing Adolphus's wife finally break down. The *them* in this scenario was anyone but a Busch.

Adolphus, meanwhile, was checked out. Christi remembers him sitting in a rocking chair, staring at a little television, tuning our mom and sisters out. He didn't speak to anybody. I had never seen this as odd, until Christi pointed it out.

At that first meeting, Christi didn't speak unless she was spoken to, and I didn't blame her. Christi didn't feel liked, which was so different from what I saw on the farm—everyone adored her there. Even my brother and our friends had a thing for her. This pompous air was so new to her. She didn't come from a family like this. She was polite when they talked to her, but she mostly just observed—and what she saw wasn't pretty.

"Billy, none of this is normal," she told me. "People do not behave like this." Christi likes to say that I had put blinders on because I didn't want to ruffle any feathers.

Mom would often have dinner parties and invite lots of people, including "suitable young women" for me—and she'd do this right in front of Christi. It was cruel and, quite frankly, crazy. But this was all for show. She knew Christi was right for me. In fact, I think she knew that Christi was tough enough to take on the likes of the Busches.

My mom could behave pretentiously in front of others, but one-on-one, she could be kind. On one occasion when Christi and I were engaged and living together, she came to Florida to watch polo. Mom took Christi shopping on Worth Avenue in Palm Beach and bought her a beautiful sweater. On another occasion, Christi was seriously having second thoughts about marrying, not because she didn't love me, but because of my tumultuous family. She and Mom went out for a walk. Christi assured Mom she wasn't marrying me for the money and suggested that calling the wedding off may be the best thing.

To Christi's shock (and mine), Mom said, "You should get married. You absolutely should get married. It's going to happen. You're perfect for him. He needs you."

Christi recalls it being a very tender and sweet moment. Since no one else was around, Christi also knew Mom was being sincere. There was no one for her to put on airs in front of. Christi recalls her being very kind, as if she was a completely different person. For a brief moment, Christ thought my mother was her friend.

But as soon as she was around other people, specifically my sisters, Christi noticed her personality turn, and she began to belittle her again. Now it was Christi who didn't know whether she was coming or going. And she could sense very clearly what I had been dealing with most of my childhood. I had been so removed from what was "real" or "normal" for so long that I had no idea just how erratic Mom's behavior was. From that point on, we were both always keenly aware that we needed to be each other's reality check.

It was clear to Christi, though, just how deep the dysfunction went, and if she was going to build a life with me, it would involve a new set of rules. She knew she wasn't going to get the support she needed from my side of the family. She wasn't going to open herself up to the type of ridicule and criticism the other in-laws suffered from. She would be no one's "beck-and-call girl" nor someone to laugh at.

Early on, she refused to go to many of the family events. Opting to sit out dinners with the family, she'd say, "You go out to the farm with your family. You should be with your family. I just don't feel like that's fun for me if they're not going to be nice. I'm not going to do that to myself."

Of course, this did her no favors in their eyes. They thought she didn't care enough about them, and they weren't used to people not bowing down and worshipping them. They all surrounded themselves with people who were going to tell them they were the greatest, the best. They did this because they liked to have control, and for the first time in their lives, they couldn't control someone. Christi was her own woman. And I loved her for it.

In 1991, when it was time to send the invitations out for our wedding, my sister Trudy said she would handle ordering them. When we got the invitations back from the printer, they read, "Gertrude Busch is pleased to give her son William Busch away to Christina Myszak." Christi's parents were so hurt by those invitations. Even I, who didn't know to get down on one knee, knew that traditionally it's the bride's parents who give their daughter away to the groom.

Christi didn't raise a fuss, but once again, she was left cleaning up the emotional wreckage with her parents that was created by my family's lack of empathy.

———

Despite all the ups and downs, on May 11, 1991, Christi and I were married in a beautiful ceremony on Grant's Farm at St. Hubert's, the chapel Dad gave to Mom as a gift when I was born. Immediately following the ceremony, as the sun was setting, Christi and I boarded the coach pulled by four shining bay horses. We coached through the Deer Park, toasting our bond with champagne. The reception was held at the Big House, and many animals were brought down for the party, including Clydesdales, elephants, macaws, and camels. We ate, drank, and danced to live music as we celebrated the night away.

We had spent days and nights before we got married fantasizing about how we would spend the rest of our lives together. I would often tell her our wedding would be in Switzerland, in a chapel in the mountains. Even though the details were a bit off, my dreams of marrying Christi had come true, and I couldn't imagine living my life without her.

We spent part of our honeymoon in Switzerland, where for a few days we could also enjoy Mom's company miles from the world that she had to put on a show for.

I think Mom saw a lot of herself in Christi. Mom was in her early twenties when she married Dad. Christi was just twenty-three. They both came from a middle-class background, and both married into this family dynasty. On top of that, Mom had four stepchildren her age to contend with, a larger-than-life husband she had to entertain for, and kids of her own to raise.

It was clear to me that Mom was projecting a lot of her own marriage and past trauma onto Christi. But while Mom's generation did things without saying a word, Christi's generation spoke their minds. Not long after we were married, my mom was drinking quite a bit one night while we were out to dinner at a local restaurant in St. Louis. She was with her new(ish) boyfriend, Buck, and we were all sitting there when an older gentleman and his twentysomething wife sat down next to us. Mom walked over to this man and said, "Why are you with this young girl? What about somebody that's your age? What about somebody like me? What the hell's the matter with you?"

The poor guy was so taken aback. I recognized him as a distributor owner and knew he was a very wealthy and successful guy. I could see how shocked he was. And his wife was about to cry.

The rest of the dinner took a nosedive. It was clear that seeing an older man with a younger woman had triggered my mother, no doubt because she was once a young wife too.

Later that night, driving home, apropos of nothing, she turned to Christi and said, "Your husband *should be* cheating on you."

"Why would I want to be married to somebody who's going to cheat on me?" Christi replied. "Why would you want that for me? Because it happened to you? You would want that for your son? You would want that for somebody else in the family? I mean it clearly didn't sit well with you. You're upset. So why?"

At that point, my mom broke down and explained how my dad was with my godmother, whom we called Aunt Marie, on the day I was being born in the hospital. When he finally showed up, she heartbreakingly went off on my father and explained that he didn't come up to see her after giving birth to me because he was with Aunt Marie. She was so upset.

Christi wouldn't let it rest. "That's not the way it's supposed to be! Don't you understand? I don't know why you would want that for anybody else!"

By now we had arrived home and were in the garage, and the two women I loved the most in this world were going at it pretty heavily. Buck had to step in to get them to stop. I couldn't take it and went into the house.

That argument sealed the deal though. I don't think my mother had ever doubted Christi's love for me, but she definitely respected her after that. No one ever had given it back to her the way Christi could and did. She never messed with Christi again.

When we found out Christi was pregnant with our first child— our son Billy—I was so happy. We were finally starting our own family.

Even though my wife and Mom learned to understand each other, my siblings were still on that vicious cycle of dysfunction. When Billy was a baby, my sister Trudy invited us out to her farm in Herman, Missouri. At one point, she asked Christi to go to the store with her to get dinner. As they were driving through the farm, Christi says Trudy became cold and silent.

Trying to break the ice, Christi said, "Trudy, your farm is so beautiful. Everything is so perfect."

Trudy looked at Christi and screamed, "Don't you dare! It took ten years before I got this farm, and you will not have anything like this!" She went on and on, railing at Christi. Suddenly, Trudy pulled up to the chapel along the road, cut the engine, and went in and prayed.

She then got back in the car and drove to the grocery store. She never spoke another word to Christi.

When Christi came back to the farm, she was visibly shaken. She asked to leave right then and there. "There is no point even trying with these people. This is bipolar bullshit." And she wanted none of it—for herself, for me, for our son Billy.

I don't know if Trudy had a bad day or what happened before Christi got in the car with her. People always have their reasons why they snap that have little to do with who they snap at. I think Trudy had to grow up too fast, had to take care of all of us kids when our mom was away, and was taught never to express her emotions. I am not making excuses for her, or for her behavior, only saying that I understand it in a way that only those who have been raised in the same dysfunction can.

For years, especially following my father's passing, we siblings had various fallings-out. Adolphus and I were supposed to have shared Belleau Farm. In his will, our father left it to both of us, but when Christi and I tried to visit the farm, Adolphus and his wife wouldn't let us in the house. They wouldn't even let us take a drive on the property in the Jeep that belonged to the farm. It was insane. They all put property over their relationships. They were all so worried that someone was going "take" what was "theirs." Even if it wasn't "theirs." Adolphus also thought he was the rightful heir to the Big House, and when we didn't allow him to take it over (because nowhere in the will did it say that he was the rightful heir), he became incredibly bitter toward us.

We started separating ourselves. Like Christi said, there seemed to be no point in making an effort as we were clearly the only ones trying. We also decided to do things differently. Mainly, we didn't want our kids to be raised by servants like I was. If we were going to have kids, we were going to raise them ourselves. Our primary goal was to make sure they would be functional and good human beings.

We were there emotionally for our kids. Christi understood their emotional needs inherently, in a way I never really could. She has this very mothering, nurturing way about her. She cares for and loves our kids more than anything in the world. From day one, she has made sure that our kids were my priority too. They came first. Plain and simple. That's just what you do. If you decide to bring kids into this world, you have to put them first and forgo a lot of other things in life.

When we got married, we both saw it as a blessing that we were able to stay home with the kids as much as possible. She laughs, "I married someone with money. I didn't look at it as a time to go, 'Whoo-hoo, I am going to travel the world, go shopping, throw parties, and leave my kids with someone else.' I looked at it this way: 'I have money that affords me a life where I don't have to work, and that lets me be with my kids.' I want to be with them as much as possible."

One of the other conscious decisions I made was to just be present. Not only physically but mentally and emotionally. No more checking out. No more leaving the garage when things got too heated. I realized the most important thing I could do for my kids was just to be there for them—whether it was at a sporting event or a rough day at school. My parents were not able to come to my high school graduation. I can't imagine missing an occasion like that for my kids.

Raising seven children isn't easy. It's busy. It's hectic. But Christi and I wouldn't change it for the world. We always say, "Seven is heaven." One of the things we often hear from others that makes us proud is how down-to-earth, respectful, and genuine each of our kids are. They are all hard workers, and besides our beer company, Busch Family Brewing & Distilling LLC, they are all involved with our other family businesses: Busch Production Co.—which includes our reality show and a weekly radio show called *Behind the Busch*—Béatus perfume, Geist Gear LLC, and Busch Family Real Estate LLC. They also actively participate in the numerous charities the family's involved with.

Our oldest, Billy, started Geist Gear LLC, a camouflage apparel and activewear company. He learned the meaning of hard work from five years of playing on the Ole Miss football team. Haley, our oldest daughter, has acted in, produced, and directed movies and TV shows. She is now very involved with real estate development and hospitality. Abbey was a fashion major in college and has done some modeling and fashion shows. She promotes our perfume line, Béatus, and is also very much involved with real estate. Gussie, our middle child, played football for the University of Alabama, where he won a national championship. After college he went on to play polo as a professional, winning several national tournaments. He's active in real estate as well, namely in managing the Busch Family Real Estate Companies, Red Hotel. Grace rides competitively, showing jumping horses nationally. When she's not participating in world-class competitions, she enjoys spending time with her horses. Maddie attends college at Parsons School of Design. She intends to design her own clothing line one day. She has also worked in the modeling arena. Peter, our number seven, is still in high school and is eager to jump into the business world upon graduation. As our youngest, he has witnessed a lot of the dos and don'ts of being in business. He has already made some impressive real estate investments.

Each of our kids is different, and they each have different needs, personalities, activities, talents, and dreams. Even now that many are grown, nothing makes us happier than when we are all together. The thing that used to drive Christi crazy about me was that I was always childlike. There is an old saying in psychology circles that you're as old as your first trauma. In so many ways, I will always be five years old at heart. I will forever be the child whose family left him behind while they were at Disneyland. I was alone in a bed, wishing I could be with them. I am also a fifteen-year-old whose sister died and who was never allowed or shown how to grieve. But, in many more ways, that childlike quality has been a blessing. I have enjoyed playing with my kids—because I still feel like a kid. I'd be the first one to jump in the ball pits. Ours is the house that all our kids' friends want to be at. We have never met some of these kids' parents, but their children have spent weeks with us. I get it. We've made a home here for our kids.

But it's not all fun and games. We have had high expectations for our kids. We follow the phrase from the Gospel of Luke (12:48), which says that to whom much is given, much will be required. We want our kids to know the importance of giving back. Christi and I take the responsibility of raising children seriously. We very consciously did everything completely opposite to how I was raised and tried to give our kids as "normal" a life as possible, as opposed to a pretentious life. When I had any of my nieces and nephews in the car and they saw a sign for Anheuser-Busch, one of them invariably would brag, "We own that." Our kids did not say those things. They did not even know we owned Grant's Farm until they were older. And they only found out because a friend of theirs said, "You know you own Grant's Farm, right?" Our response was, "No, you don't." Because that was the truth. It belonged to me and my siblings, not them.

Christi and I are glad to this day that we did that because when Anheuser-Busch was sold, it didn't affect our kids to the extent it did other family members, whose identity was linked to being owners. We knew we had to move on and create a new legacy or continue a legacy in a new way. Grant's Farm and Anheuser-Busch were not our identities. We had a new set of rules. And this time, family truly reigned. Not just our name. Not just our property. Not just our identities as "Busches."

We believe that the most important legacy we can leave in this world is children who have strong morals and values and contribute positively to society. We've worked really hard to make sure our children know *our family* was what mattered. Because, when it came down to it, when the going got tough, my siblings seemed to forget that.

Part Four

ALL IN THE FAMILY

Chapter Thirteen
THE DYNASTY FALLS, BUT THE LEGACY CONTINUES

Even though it's well known now that the Anheuser-Busch Company was bought in 2008 by InBev, a Brazilian-run Belgian company, for me, the beginning of the end of the Anheuser-Busch family dynasty started years before, right around the time Christi and I married in 1991. While Christi and I were dating, we sold our Homestead, Florida, distributorship and purchased a much larger one in Houston, with Adolphus and Andy. I moved from St. Louis to Houston, and Christi stayed with me when she could as I helped manage the operations. As I mentioned earlier, August III approved the sale from an old friend of my mom and dad, Bill Georges. At that time, there were five partners in our group. Adolphus insisted that we essentially give one-sixth of the business over to a new partner who had no experience in the beer business—a man who happened to be his best friend. We didn't need him financially, as he didn't bring equity to the table, but just to appease Adolphus, we agreed to it. And Adolphus was smart. He knew his friend would vote for anything Adolphus was in favor of.

Over the years, we were doing well and were gaining market share. By 1991 Adolphus, Andy, and I were forced to sell because of a Texas alcohol law prohibiting brewery family members from owning distributorships. No one knew about this law when we purchased the distributorship, but because we started cutting into the Miller Brewing Company's profits, they began looking for ways to get rid of us. They found a loophole in the law that would require us to divest ourselves of all Anheuser-Busch interests. This meant we would have to sell our Anheuser-Busch stock and end the lease on Grant's Farm with Anheuser-Busch. For months we fought this law in court but to no avail. Finally, the courts ordered us to sell or divest ourselves of everything pertaining to Anheuser-Busch. We had no other choice but to sell the distributorship.

Unbeknownst to Andy and me, Adolphus had already worked out a deal with two of the partners where he would stay on as a secret consultant. It was clear that the only people who'd make out on the deal would be Adolphus, his friend, and our other partner. My brother Andy and I and the other original partner who was with us when we purchased the Homestead distributorship had to go toe-to-toe with them to get the full value of what the distributorship was worth. Even though Adolphus and his two allies got what they wanted, Adolphus was still pissed at us because we didn't do exactly what he told us to do. The Houston distributorship sold for a billion dollars in 2019. Not a bad profit.

The way I see it, because our dad was so old, Adolphus always felt like he was the family's patriarch. And for many years, we allowed it—especially Andy and me. We were the youngest and looked up to Adolphus. He took on the responsibility of being a father figure, but he took it too far for too long. If he didn't get his way, he didn't want anything to do with us. That's how it went at the shooting lodge too. He felt entitled to everything because, as the oldest, he felt he simply deserved it, even though our dad left it to both of us. He was also bitter about Grant's Farm. After our dad died, he just assumed he would take over. That didn't happen, and it made even him more resentful.

The last straw for him, where I was concerned, was the distributorship. Nothing was ever just business for him; it was personal. He felt he had a God-given right to be able to control us and be the boss of the family. He had always been this way. But after our mom left, both he and Trudy stepped in as the de facto adults in our family. They both felt the need to call the shots, and as we became adults, that didn't change. In fact, he was so mad at me about the distributorship that he didn't come to my wedding.

After I sold the distributorship, I focused on the Bud Light polo team for several years, winning many major tournaments in the United States together with my brother Andy, while Christi and I raised our growing family. In 1991 Andy and I even beat the undefeated all-pro polo team that Adolphus sponsored at the US Open in the finals. This was the first time in the over hundred-year history that a team with two sponsors and two pros won the US Open. Adolphus was such a competitive son of a gun, and this defeat was a hard pill for him to swallow. The distance between us just continued to grow. It took years for him to get over it—in fact, I don't think he ever has.

For the most part, we Busch kids all went our separate ways, only occasionally gathering at the Big House to keep the traditions going as we each focused on our own families. Andy married and moved to California. Peter continued running his Budweiser distributorship in Fort Pierce, Florida. Adolphus lived out at Belleau (the shooting lodge) and kept to himself, finally achieving the privacy he so craved but never got when we were kids living in the fishbowl that was Grant's Farm. Beaty headed out to Virginia, and Trudy lived nearby, but we kept our distance. Christi and I moved just outside the city limits of St. Louis, and we raised our kids there, sending them to Catholic schools and trying to be as involved as possible with all of them.

After our son Billy was born, my relationship with my half sister Elizabeth grew stronger than ever after years of not speaking. Christi urged me to take Billy, who was just born, over to see her. Although I was hesitant due to not talking to her for all those years, the proud dad came out in me, and I took Billy over to meet his aunt. As fate would have it, that began a relationship that would last until she died years later. It turns out the half sister who sided with August III became my closest and most supportive sibling of all.

In 2002 August III broke with tradition and handed the company's reins over to his son August IV. We all knew it was not a good move. My great-grandfather and grandfather wouldn't have just handed the company to the oldest. They all had to prove themselves capable of leading the company before taking over. Case in point—my father and his own brother were fiercely competitive until my grandfather's death, trying to prove themselves to him. The company was passed down to Adolphus III because not only was he the oldest but he proved himself competent.

The irony of August III passing the company on to his son is not lost on me. August III *took* the company from our dad, ending the legacy of passing the company on to the most competent son. Maybe he believed he was preserving some legacy by passing the company on to his firstborn son, but he, himself, hadn't earned the right.

For the next few years, we watched as Anheuser-Busch went downhill under August IV's leadership. We all had heard that he had a drug problem and was probably not fit for leadership; it was a well-reported and documented fact. He had also crashed a car while at college in Arizona and abandoned the scene of the crime—leaving behind his passenger, Michelle Frederick, just twenty-two at the time, to die. When he made horrible life choices, his father always found a way to get him out of trouble (something our dad also did as well). But when it came to disastrous business decisions, August III's hands were tied. He couldn't help his son, and the drug problem continued.

Dad never tolerated illegal drug use of any kind. He was totally and emphatically against it and would threaten to kick any of his kids who used drugs out of the family. In fact, he was against drunkenness or drinking until one became inebriated. Above all, in the alcohol industry, Dad knew that the leader of Anheuser-Busch had to always be of sound mind. Although Dad could drink a lot, I never saw him drunk. August III knew this and must have known Dad would have never handed August IV the reins of the company if he was a drug user.

I had only heard stories anecdotally about what was going on inside the company. I had no way of knowing what was happening within the walls of the brewery since I wasn't there. But among family, friends, and the St. Louis rumor mill, we heard about August IV's struggle with addiction and his troubles managing the company.

That being said, he has a kind heart. He was always generous when it came to giving my family access to Busch-owned entertainment and theme parks. We always appreciated that about him. And we all recognized he had his struggles too. I understood that better than anyone. He was raised and groomed to take over the brewery, and he didn't have a father figure as much as he had a boss. He longed for a father, and I could relate to that longing in so many ways. His mom and dad divorced, and his father remarried and had two other kids. The competition between August IV and his half brother, Steven, was tough on him.

Steven was a very educated person, experienced at the brewery, and a bright guy. He was also working at the brewery and people loved him. He was an introvert, whereas August IV was an extrovert and loved to party. August IV was insecure about his young half brother getting the reins as they grew up (just like his father felt about his own half brothers). I even heard from my half sister Elizabeth that August IV was so worried his brother might get the company, he tried to run Steven off the road while they were racing around the switchbacks on the treacherous and windy Road to Hana in Maui. Later August IV told me it was actually Steven who tried to run *him* off the road. Either way you look at it, it was a very competitive situation between two brothers vying for control.

Like most of the world, when I read that there was a good chance that InBev might buy Anheuser-Busch, I wondered, *How can this be? Anheuser-Busch is the largest beer company in the world. There is no one else big enough to buy them!* Well, InBev apparently was. Anheuser-Busch stock had been stagnant for years, and to make matters worse, the market was crashing at the time. The Anheuser-Busch stock hadn't budged for ten years and not at all since August IV had taken over. But it was set to decline. August III had passed on buying international breweries like Carlsberg, a Danish multinational brewer, and other international brewing conglomerates that were low-hanging fruit ripe for picking.

Purchases like this would have taken some control away from August III, and anyone who knew him and the size of his ego could easily understand why he killed those deals. Meanwhile, two up-and-coming brewing conglomerates—a European group called Interbrew and a South American group called Ambev—merged to become InBev, creating the new largest brewery in the world.

When the deal went through, I read how it happened in the newspapers. Somehow, Carlos Brito, head of InBev, convinced August IV to allow InBev to distribute their beers within the Anheuser-Busch wholesaler network. This gave Brito the chance to look at Anheuser-Busch's financials. Of course, InBev pored over those documents and had all the ammunition they needed to swoop in and take over.

In an effort to stop the sale, August IV started cutting expenses to raise the value of the company. He had seen how wasteful his father had become by having the company purchase a large fleet of some of the most expensive private planes. He and his father had a huge argument when he announced that he was going to significantly downsize August III's precious fleet. Ironic, considering August III claimed our father wasn't fit to lead the brewery due to his "wasteful" spending on the boats. The strategy didn't work, but August IV had one last plan.

Anheuser-Busch owned half of the Mexican brewery that made Corona and Modelo. He made a deal to purchase the remaining 50 percent of that brewery, which would have made Anheuser-Busch too pricey to buy. The board was willing to go along with the plan, but by then August III had come to fully realize his son's problems, and he was smart enough to see that if the InBev deal was stopped, he would be exposed to lawsuits from stockholders who would have missed out on the cash windfall of the sale, and in the suit, it would have come out that he and the board instead turned the company over to a drug addict. So August III convinced the board of directors, whom he had handpicked, to approve the sale to InBev. Just as important, as a result, he had the opportunity to structure the deal with InBev so that he stood to gain a lot of money, essentially making himself a billionaire. All things considered, he must have felt the family tradition was worth losing at this point. August III alone was responsible for ending the dynasty.

Dad had given us several thousand shares in the company each Christmas with a letter wishing us a Merry Christmas and signed *your loving dad*. As a kid I didn't realize the value of what this gift meant. All I knew was he made a point of telling us to always hold on to the stock and that one day it would be very valuable. He always said: "Hold on to the A-B shares, Billy. Never sell." In 2008 it looked like the market was going down and everything was crashing. Even Warren Buffett sold his shares. Our trustee's best advice was to sell. I held on. And when I began to have my doubts, Christi urged me not to sell. Our decision became: "We lived by the sword, we'll die by the sword." We knew August IV was not a competent leader, and the stock would definitely tank if the InBev deal fell through. We had the most to lose of all the siblings by holding on to so much stock. Instead of asking, "What would Adolphus do?" during those stressful weeks, we asked, "What would Gussie do?" My father would never have sold. He would have bet on the name Anheuser-Busch. So we held out. If my family was already annoyed with Christi and me at this point, I am sure they were beyond jealous and resentful when they saw the price of the stock jump to seventy dollars a share. In the end, InBev bought Anheuser-Busch for $52 billion. At the conclusion of the deal, Christi and I made a lot of money. We had followed Dad's advice, and it had paid off.

It was bittersweet, of course. On the one hand, the family legacy my father had fought so hard for was now in the hands of a foreign company, but on the other hand, the Anheuser-Busch name would remain forever. And in the end, we still had Grant's Farm. As part of the deal, InBev would now lease it from us.

Another bright spot, I thought, was that I could finally fulfill a dream I'd always had—and shared with my father: running a brewery myself. Since, for obvious reasons, I was never going to be able to run Anheuser-Busch, the only way I could ever become a brewer was if I went out on my own. I loved the beer business. I helped manage two successful distributorships, working in operations daily. I even drove a beer truck and worked in the warehouse. I enjoyed meeting with customers, bar owners, grocery store owners, and people from all walks of life to talk about our beer. I could see why my father loved being on the road so much, entertaining wholesalers and customers of all kinds. It was fun.

Most people bleed blood; I felt I bled beer. It was in my DNA. Even though InBev had our company, it didn't have us—the Busch family *or* the Busch name. That would always be ours. They would never have our history either. I didn't want to lose the legacy and tradition that my father and forefathers had worked so hard for. My grandfather loved his wife and family above all else, and he loved Grant's Farm, yet he died for the company. I had witnessed my father's determination and saw all that he had built—amusement parks, a global company, and a winning baseball franchise. We had inherited one of the most unbelievable companies this country had ever seen. The day the deal was signed, I knew he would be rolling over in his grave. Those were things I couldn't let go of. But two things can be true at the same time: we could mourn the end of Anheuser-Busch as we knew it, and we could celebrate the opportunity to rebuild and continue the beer-brewing legacy of our forefathers. Those were things that sustained Christi and me.

My dad was a pragmatic man. Even he considered selling the company at one point. Granted, he couldn't let it go, but he was above all a businessman who seized opportunities. Now was our time to do the same. I had the money and I had the freedom. So in 2009, right after the sale was finalized, Christi and I followed our passion and family history. We launched our beer: "Kräftig," which means *powerful* in German. We had a powerful name, a powerful legacy, and we believed we were going to make one of the most powerful marks in the beer industry since Anheuser-Busch was launched over one hundred and fifty years earlier. This was our turn to start our own beer business, with our own family. It was an exciting time to say the least.

I knew right away who I *wasn't* going to ask to be my partners: my siblings. I had already been in business with those guys and saw how that turned out. I had no intention of repeating past mistakes. At this point, we weren't even getting along for a number of reasons. Christi and I were dealing with an incredibly painful private issue and coping the best we could. We were going to extraordinary lengths to keep a family member sober, and several of my siblings went behind our backs and drank with and enabled this family member. It was impossible for Christi and me to wrap our minds around this, especially after everything we'd done to keep this family member safe. To this day, it is too difficult to discuss. In the end, none of us saw the issue the same way. And it ripped us apart all over again. Whatever hope we had for reparations and reconciliation was torn apart then and would remain that way for years.

So when I started looking for business partners, I started talking to some of the executives who had been let go from Anheuser-Busch after the takeover. I thought they'd be knowledgeable about the business and would understand the legacy I was trying to protect. I thought they could help me create the new dynasty.

Just like my great-grandfather, we were starting from scratch. Several top executives from Anheuser-Busch joined me to launch a new beer company in my own name—William K. Busch Brewing Co. The problem I didn't anticipate was that "executives" (even unemployed ones) didn't want to take start-up pay, work start-up hours, or do things a new and different way. Not only that, but they wanted free equity in the company, which I granted, believing it would motivate them to work harder. Boy, was I wrong. What I got was a lot of corporate drama, which is the worst thing about running a company.

They were pretty entitled. They thought very highly of themselves.

Add to that, we were launching a business at one of the worst times in economic history and going up against some significant opposition from competitors in the emerging craft beer industry. Kräftig was not only our first beer, it was also the first beer to be brewed by anyone with a Busch name since InBev took over Anheuser-Busch. I wanted to create a beer that could compete with national brands, including those that had made our family famous. The goal was to brew up to two million barrels a year, build a brewing facility—which I'd hoped would be on Grant's Farm—and restore my family's legacy. It was, I realize now, a monumental task. For one, we were up against InBev, who shipped nearly 102 million barrels a year in the United States and had a stronghold on distribution. I thought if we could get just a 2 percent market share in the United States, we would be well over that two-million-barrel mark.

Though my family had been in the beer business for 150 years, and I had worked at a distributorship, I had never run a brewery before or been at the helm. It was an eye-opening experience. I consulted with master brewers all around the world, tried ten different recipes, and followed all the German purity laws by keeping the lager to just four ingredients. I chose a German name that means *powerful* and is used to describe someone who overcomes insurmountable obstacles. That was who I was, someone who overcame obstacles, and I wanted our company to be an underdog of sorts—to overcome our loss and take back our family legacy and name. The Busch family was nothing if not resilient, and I wanted our name to show that. I didn't just want to be a local craft beer; I wanted Kräftig to be a premium mainstream beer. I wanted to sell it at a price point of seven dollars for a six-pack—less than, say, Sam Adams or Sierra Nevada, but more expensive than Budweiser. I had high hopes. I was excited about building a business I could share with my own kids.

When we released Kräftig in 2011, we had a huge rollout event with ice sculptures of our logo at Forest Park. We invited the media, and all of them showed up. We lit up the territories we were in with billboards, points of sale, and advertisements. Almost immediately, we received incredible feedback that people loved our beer. Wholesalers everywhere wanted to carry Kräftig. *Forbes* magazine did a big story on us, and I was on its cover. Every local news station and newspaper put us on the front page. One headline was: "The Busches are back in the beer business." I did TV and radio ads myself.

We sponsored concerts, car racing, and almost every event we could where drinking beer is popular. We hired a sales team to hit the streets and gave them a spending allowance to buy customers our beer. The giveaways were tremendous and cost a lot of money, but that was all a part of the extensive marketing-and-sales program we used to help us reach our goals.

Little did I know that I had a target on my back. The distributors called it the "Kill Bill" target. Anheuser-Busch/InBev asked their managers and distributors to do everything they could to disrupt our sales. They would go into restaurants and bars and take down our signage and erase a promotion we may have had with an account. They would bribe owners with tickets to the Super Bowl, World Series, and other prime sporting events. They did this almost everywhere we sold our beer. It was malicious, and they had the money and wherewithal to stop us. I often think that if I had any other name, I could have launched my beer without so much resistance.

Despite how we were met in the marketplace, we were crushing it in taste tests. Between 2011 and 2019, we won the US Open Beer Competition eight times. It wasn't just about the flavor either. It was how it looked when we poured it into the glass. It foamed beautifully; it had perfect lacing. It had the perfect level of carbonation. It had a wonderful hop-and-barley smell. And yes, it tasted delicious. We won almost every competition we entered. Our standards were excellent. My dad would have loved it.

But we couldn't make inroads with the distributors no matter how hard we tried. Due to our quality standards, I would not allow old beer to be sold (even if it was one day over its limit). Once it's out of code, the taste and drinkability are just not the same. So when sales slowed, old beer that sat in the marketplace had to be picked up and thrown away. And we were hemorrhaging money on marketing and sponsorships. I place a lot of the blame on myself.

I learned a lot of hard lessons in those first few years of brewing. I learned you can't really rely on anybody else. You've got to own your decisions and know the business backward and forward, just as my forefathers were taught. In so many ways, I went in blind. And I let my enthusiasm and my trust in others get the best of me. I let myself believe in the capabilities of men who had worked at and inherited a successful brewing company with an established name. They were used to manning an ocean liner going full speed ahead, and I was putting them on a small sailboat and sending them out to sea. They had no idea how to make it float, let alone how to sail. They thought they knew everything when working for a well-oiled machine with all the resources imaginable. In reality, they knew nothing about a start-up on a shoestring budget. But I was nothing if not persistent and believed we could persevere. I believed 100 percent that this was what my father would have wanted. We were doing something great. I wasn't getting any younger, and I didn't want to just be part of a dying legacy. I wanted to do something meaningful and have it count. So, despite all my better judgment, I kept going.

I was working my ass off and taking time away from my family—traveling all over Missouri, Kansas, Wisconsin, Illinois, and Texas. I had a lot of empathy for my dad, grandfather, and great-grandfather. Running a brewery wasn't for the faint of heart. It was grueling, exhausting, and mostly thankless. Even knowing all the financial concerns we were up against, the executives asked for raises and more free equity. I was paying all these guys well, yet they weren't delivering and were never happy. They just wanted more and more. The more I did for people, the less grateful they seemed. Still, I didn't drop my standards. The beer and my customers were the most important thing, and I wanted to make my family proud. After all, what would Gussie do?

Gussie would turn a profit.

I started to clean house, but I had to pay them for the equity I had given them. And I started to look at other ways to make the company profitable. What did my dad do? He used Grant's Farm. So, I thought, that's what we could do.

Over the years, we siblings had come together when it came to the farm and the family legacy. Despite all we had put each other through, I was ready to forgive them, and I thought they would all be behind me as I hoped to keep Grant's Farm in the family and continue our brewing legacy.

What could go wrong?

Chapter Fourteen
THE FIGHT OVER GRANT'S FARM

Grant's Farm was something we (the family) leased to Anheuser-Busch for marketing and event purposes. When InBev took over Anheuser-Busch, they took over the lease. However, the ownership of Grant's Farm, its animals, and the Big House was left in a trust to us six kids—Adolphus, Trudy, Beaty, Peter, Andy, and me. As beneficiaries of the trust, if one of us died, their portion would be left to their family's estate. We were all getting older, and around 2012 to 2014, all of us started contemplating what to do with the Grant's Farm Trust before one of us died. During this time, I thought it would be a great business move if I offered to buy the farm outright because I knew it would be a great place to set up a brewery and entertain, just as our father had done before me. He opened the farm to the public in 1954 and immediately realized the PR benefit as well as the brand loyalty it created for Anheuser-Busch and its products. With this knowledge, my father opened other breweries around the country surrounded by animal parks. He truly was a marketing genius. Above all, however, I adored the farm. I had worked on it my entire life, and unlike Adolphus, who hated living in a place visited by the public, I enjoyed that aspect of it. I knew what went into caring for all the animals, and I had a deep reverence for our family legacy. In my father's will, he made it clear that his greatest wish was that one or more of his children would buy and keep Grant's Farm in the family, though he didn't specify *who* that should be.

Not surprisingly, with the exception of Adolphus, my siblings objected to my bid. They preferred to sell the property to the St. Louis Zoo. What shocked me was that Adolphus, who always had difficulties with me, was in my corner during this fight. Adolphus is a lot of things, but he's not stupid. He knew a good business deal when he saw one. I also think he couldn't stand Trudy, Beaty, and Andy and really wanted to stick it to them. Adolphus looked out for Adolphus. And since our family's alliances changed daily, based on who was pissed off with whom, I knew his allegiance could change at any minute.

I had created a business plan, which I presented in a beautiful wooden binder, that would prove to be profitable if we could put the brewery on the land we'd inherited. If need be, we could also charge a small admission to help cover the costs. To make them all feel comfortable, Christi and I also granted them first rights of refusal. We wanted to give them the security of knowing that we would keep the farm in the family if I couldn't make the business work. We basically said they could buy the farm back for exactly what they sold it to me for. There was literally no risk at all for them to sell to me. They would get the same amount of money from me that they would get from the zoo, we all would keep it in the family, and if things didn't work out, they could buy it back from me for the same amount. It was a perfect business deal.

And yet, they still all decided they didn't want me to buy it.

Even though InBev now owned Anheuser-Busch and my siblings didn't technically have anything to do with the company, my siblings claimed that InBev didn't want any beer consumed on the premises than Anheuser-Busch. Technically, while InBev leased about two hundred acres around Grant's Farm from us, they had absolutely no input on what we did to the twenty-two acres of the private estate and the Big House, which we all controlled outright. Barring the serving of any beer other than Anheuser-Busch on the twenty-two acres was just an excuse. What it came down to was that my siblings didn't like me and Christi. There is no other way to make sense of it because Christi and I made every concession there was and an offer no one could refuse.

Part of the reason was they still bought into the fairy tale—the "magic" of the name Anheuser-Busch. My siblings couldn't separate themselves from that name, even though it wasn't part of the family anymore. Budweiser was part of their identity. Even though InBev now owned Anheuser-Busch, they didn't want any beer—including our beer, Kräftig—competing against it. They didn't realize that InBev didn't care about Grant's Farm the way Christi and I did. For InBev, it was just a marketing tool, and because of the cost, Grant's Farm was deteriorating and no longer being maintained to its previous standard.

I will say that Peter was on my side for a time as well, but ultimately he changed his mind when he "saw my business plan." It has been reported and often said within the family that Peter was the "smartest businessman" among us Busches because he owned such a successful distributorship. Personally, I don't think his change of heart had anything to do with smarts but, rather, with rivalry and jealousy. Running a well-oiled Budweiser machine that was basically handed to you doesn't require a high degree of intelligence, especially back in those days when we all owned distributorships. There was such a huge demand for Budweiser back then. It was the kind of business that would make anybody look like they're a great business leader. I should know; I ran two successful distributorships.

Running a start-up brewery was different and took a different set of skills. It was a hell of a lot harder. Don't get me wrong, I still loved every aspect of running my brewery. I loved going to concerts, Summerfests, Oktoberfests, and meeting the hundreds of thousands of people who visited our tents to try our beer. It was during those times that I felt most connected to my father, grandfather, and my great-grandfather. It gave me a great amount of compassion and empathy for them, especially during the lean times. I knew firsthand that it wasn't an easy business to break into. I thought, *Wouldn't it be great if people could come to Grant's Farm to taste our beer?* I had high hopes of bringing Kräftig to Grant's Farm and helping it flourish there, like my father had done with his breweries all over the country.

Of course, with any investment comes some risk. They argued they were worried that if Kräftig didn't do well or InBev pulled their lease, I wouldn't be able to cover all the expenses of running Grant's Farm and the Big House. (And they had no idea at the time that I was already losing money.) I think they thought selling to the St. Louis Zoo was a sure bet. The zoo had money and would always have the money since it was state funded.

However, what is still striking to me to this day is that they all knew Dad's explicit wishes. He made it clear in his will that he wanted one or more of his kids to own it outright and keep it in the family. Christi and I were the ones willing to do that, and we gave them every opportunity to join us and be investors. If nothing else, we gave them the assurance that they would always have the ability to visit the farm. The last thing we would ever do is take their childhood home away from them. But they decided they'd rather deny our dad's wishes than let me be the "lord of the manor," as they so often put it. It was a jealousy problem. I was the last person in the family they wanted running things. It was definitely personal. Because, to be fair, no one in the family knew and loved the farm like I did or wanted to buy it and keep it in the family. There was also no one else in the family willing to carry on the family tradition of running a brewery. Additionally, Christi and I were dedicated to keeping the farm looking beautiful, which because of cost-cutting measures, InBev was no longer doing. Also, we weren't going to do what the zoo proposed, which was to put up walls and add extensive amounts of concrete that would completely change the feel of the farm.

After years of wrangling for control, it came down to the wire in 2017. The media in Missouri and even national news highlighted the controversy between the Busch family members and Grant's Farm.

This was great drama, and it made for front-page news. Public opinion began blasting my siblings and supporting me, hoping I would be granted the farm. The zoo, seeing the negative press they were getting by opposing me, decided to drop their bid to purchase Grant's Farm. With no other buyer than me, our chances of purchasing the farm became even better.

However, my four siblings, who at this time were ready to walk away and sell the farm, formed a "coalition" (as they called it) with our very wealthy nephew, Bob Herman, Lilly's son. Together, the "coalition" decided to buy Grant's Farm themselves. They just could not see one Busch owning Grant's Farm—or, as Trudy put it, one "lord of the manor." Once again, my family's dysfunction reared its ugly head. If I was successful, what a blow that would have been to my siblings. Their jealousy and lack of support confounded me. Why was it so hard to see siblings succeed?

The trustee, Wells Fargo, gave us all a hard deadline—it was do-or-die time. For months Wells Fargo put me through hoops. I had to come up with a legitimate business plan and prove I could get a loan. So, I got the loan from J.P. Morgan for Grant's Farm, which I had not even bought yet, and paid interest on that loan. Meanwhile, I had to deal with a lawsuit my siblings filed against me, trying to force the sale to the zoo. They ended up losing, but it still cost me a lot of money in lawyer fees. In addition, I had to take an enormous amount of time away from the beer business, which desperately required my full attention.

Finally, we got a call from Wells Fargo saying that if my four siblings—Peter, Beaty, Trudy, Andy—and nephew Bob Herman didn't come back with an offer by that afternoon, Christi and I could buy the farm. At the time, Christi, myself, and some of the kids were down in Mississippi visiting our son Billy, who was playing football for Ole Miss. All day long we never heard a thing. So, by five o'clock that day, we thought, *This is it! We got it! We got the farm!* We were already celebrating and in the middle of talking about all the great things we were going to do when we got a call.

It was Wells Fargo. They had decided to sell the farm to the coalition even though they came back with their offer hours after their "hard deadline." Their excuse was that those five had more money to sustain the farm in perpetuity than I did. Of course, we felt that Wells Fargo had betrayed us. The only solace we received from the trustee was that the five had to offer Christi and me a one-sixth partnership in Grant's Farm. An offer we extended to them if we bought Grant's Farm, but not one they would have offered to us without Wells Fargo's directive.

Before the sale, Andy and I went out for lunch. Andy said, "We want to know if you are going to be part of our coalition." (I had to laugh again—they actually called themselves a "coalition.") Then he started explaining how things would be run. "You can't serve Kräftig in the Big House, and you can't host meetings or events. We"—he meant the coalition—"are going to run things, and we've decided to run things in a democratic way. That means we will vote on everything we do in the Big House and the surrounding area."

My response was, "InBev doesn't lease the Big House or the surrounding twenty acres. We can serve anything we'd like to, so why would I not serve our beer, conduct business, and host events like I always have at the Big House for the last several years?"

He responded that he didn't want to "muddy the waters" with InBev.

"That doesn't make sense, because InBev has always respected our privacy at the house and the twenty acres and understood this part of the farm was off-limits to them," I said. "Why would I live with that? Because we're free to do exactly what we want to do on that portion of Grant's Farm." It was their way of forcing me out. Funny thing is Andy later used Grant's Farm to promote his wine, and Bob Herman served his craft beer at the Big House.

I got up from the lunch, without much protest from him, as I could see the writing on the wall.

"You're going to vote me out of everything you possibly can. It won't be fair," I said.

Later when I spoke with Christi about it, we both agreed that there was no way to continue with the family or Grant's Farm. There was more to life than constantly fighting and being outvoted and controlled on what we could or couldn't do. And when it came down to it, as painful as it was, we no longer were part of Anheuser-Busch. We had to start looking in a new direction. InBev didn't care about our house, our family, our heritage. They cared about running their business and making money, and as soon as Grant's Farm didn't seem profitable to them, they would drop the lease.

Ultimately, Adolphus and I sold our portion of Grant's Farm to the five. The only consolation was that through my negotiation efforts, we both received a million dollars more than we would have. Considering the time spent, the cost of the business plan, paying lawyers, and interest on the loan, the extra million was more of a wash than anything. Who really made out like a bandit was Adolphus, who helped create this bidding war to drive up the price on the home he desperately wanted out of.

Shortly before we closed on the sale, my family and I went to Grant's Farm to say our goodbyes to the elephants as this would be the last time we would ever see them. It was a tearful farewell as our beloved Bud wrapped his trunk around me, not wanting to let go—as if he knew this was it. As we walked away, he gave us one last trumpet. A few weeks later, we found out that Bud, who was in robust health, had died, followed over the next couple of months by Mickey and the other two elephants that lived there. To this day I believe they died of a broken heart and that was reiterated by other employees on the farm. There was no other explanation given on their cause of death.

I haven't set foot on Grant's Farm since 2017. My family and I so loved the place. It's where I met Christi, where we married, where we baptized and raised our kids. Like so many other St. Louisans, Grant's Farm was a childhood institution—in fact, my entire childhood. We were heartbroken by the loss of traditions we had come to enjoy as a family there—Christmases, graduations, New Year's Eves, and birthday parties.

Not surprisingly, InBev dropped its lease in 2020. We all knew it was coming. And surprise, surprise, my siblings have to run Grant's Farm in a way similar to what I proposed in my business plan. Everything we predicted came true, including losing Kräftig. Without the support of Grant's Farm, having a brewery on the premises, or the ability to sell our beer, we lost that too.

"Take it in the back and shoot it," Christi said to me one day. She wasn't talking about a sick horse but my business. "Billy, you've got to let this go. Let them go. We've got to cut our losses now. This is not working." The final straw for the business was when Christi and our eldest daughter, Haley, came to our management meeting to better understand why our company was still not profitable. If you know Christi, she's not one to sit quietly and be taken advantage of. She's always been one to speak up for herself and the ones she loves. When she spoke up, our highest-paid ex-Anheuser-Busch executive started yelling in her face that she was not an owner of our business and had no right to be there, much less ask questions. With a red face, he stood up, shaking his finger at her and pointing to the other ex-Anheuser-Busch execs, saying he and those guys owned the company, that Christi and Haley didn't, and that her say in running the business did not matter.

It took all I had not to punch this guy right in the nose. Christi had every right to be in this meeting. She was my partner and the person who had been with me from the conception of this business and everything in between. I couldn't stand listening to her being spoken to in such a degrading way. I was completely taken aback, and my eyes were opened to the kind of people I had working for me. I learned that, ultimately, everyone is out for themselves and their own best interest. The only ones who have your back and who you can truly rely on are your immediate family members. Looking back, I can admit that I'd lost sight of this truth and put my faith and money in the hands of others while putting my family and their opinions on the back burner. I can say now that this lesson will stick with me for the rest of my life. I never liked getting rid of people, but I must say, firing this entitled, overgrown bully was quite satisfying, to say the least.

Even though we ended up having to shut down the production of

Kräftig, we haven't given up. We're still working on new beers at Busch Family Brewing & Distilling Company, and we have no plans to give up preserving the Busch brewing family legacy.

What has been the most painful is how my family decided to treat us. Christi, my children, and I are not "allowed" on the Grant's Farm property. In fact, one of our friends went to rent an event space at Grant's Farm, and they mentioned they knew Christi and me. They were told that if the event they were having needed to have either of us on the guest list, they should pick another venue because we were not allowed on the premises. Over the years, I am sure that the siblings have all gathered, as we typically did during holidays and other family events, but we have not been invited.

As sad as this sounds, I have to admit that finally escaping the family dysfunction was one of the best things that ever happened to me. It was a relief, to be honest. I had tried my entire life to make peace with my family. I had romanticized them, but in the end, they were human, just like me. We were all pretty messed up. We had a lot to overcome in our lives, and no matter how hard we tried to make it work, we just weren't the type of family to get along.

That being said, there is not a day that goes by that I don't think about and miss the farm. It was such a massive part of my life and made me into the person I am today. It is impossible to describe the size of the loss. The happiest memories of my life happened right there on that farm—and the most tragic ones as well: losing Christina, watching our parents' marriage end, losing Anheuser-Busch, and finally letting the farm—and my family—go.

I had a new chapter—a whole book, as it turns out—to write. And this one would be mine. It would be Christi's. It would be our kids'.

The legacy continues. And I am just getting started.

Epilogue
RELEASING THE REINS

Some things from my childhood I still carry on. Like my father and mother before me, Christi and I enjoy taking carriage rides around our property together. Like Grant's Farm, our place, Blue Heron Farm, which we bought in 1997, is home to many animals. We have horses of all kinds, including miniatures, Thoroughbreds, Belgians, and of course, Clydesdales. We have a variety of farm animals, including different species of cattle, pigs, donkeys, alpacas, chickens, and sheep. We also have camels, capuchin monkeys, kinkajous, parrots, and a variety of dogs and cats. The beauty of the farm is breathtaking, with rolling hills, open meadows for planting, streams, lakes, ponds, and an abundance of hardwood and conifer trees. It will never replace Grant's Farm, but I know it holds memories that are no less precious for my children than those at Grant's Farm were for me. And like my father before me, we've opened the grounds to the public, as well as the brewery and distillery. It's truly magical and we are blessed for it. Though we don't have throngs of audiences watching as my dad and mom did, it's special all the same.

Currently, the family has been discussing doing a second season of our reality show, *The Busch Family Brewed*, but with the kids growing up and doing their own thing, it's hard to get everyone on board. It's never

easy to wrangle seven kids for any event, let alone for a show. After the
first season aired, the feedback from people who watched it was amazing. Even August IV, who loves his privacy and usually lies low, called
and said that his popularity and image had grown more positive because
of it. It showed the Busches in a positive way. We were a wholesome
family who cared about each other and our community. It was a fun
experience, and I am glad we did it.

As many fans of the show know, when Christi and I are driving the
horses, we do much of our talking about the day's events, our children,
and what really matters. We've come to believe that the legacy we leave
isn't so much about beer but our new definition of what it means to be
a family, what it means to love, what it means to dedicate your life to
something bigger than yourself. It means love, laughter, hope, and seeing
your kids' dreams as your dreams; not necessarily passing the dreams of
our ancestors on to future generations, but rather allowing future generations to rethink what is possible for their own future.

Our children are as unique and different as each one of my siblings
and I were, but unlike me and my siblings, my kids have the opportunity to imagine their lives as their own creations, to be the architects of
their own destinies, their own legacies, and to create their own identities. They can be real and not live a fairy tale.

They are free and unbridled; the family reins that were once held so
tightly no longer hold them—or me—back. We still keep a lot of the
traditions that were passed on to me. The kids—Billy Jr., Haley, Abbey,
Gussie, Grace, and Maddie—come home on holidays, some weekends,
and in the summer to enjoy our beautiful lake. And the youngest, Peter,
still lives with us.

Christi and I have so many dreams and things we want to do
and achieve in whatever time we have remaining in this life—outside of running a brewery and running a farm. Our ultimate hope
is that our children grow up knowing they are loved—have always
been loved—and that they grow into kind and contributing members of society. I know they aren't perfect. Christi and I aren't perfect
parents either. We are all human. But we have always put them first

and want them to realize that we will be there for them, no matter what. I also hope that, come what may in life, they treat each other with respect and dignity.

We are a tight family already, and I think that's because of how open we've been and how much we've communicated with each other. We raised our kids and set them up so that history won't repeat itself. Now, I know there's no way to say that it can't happen. There's always a possibility that division and hurt can erupt within families. But my one continuous prayer is that no matter what happens, they at least try to see each other's points of view. I don't think there is anything that *can't* be forgiven or salvaged, and as a believer in Jesus Christ, I believe all can be forgiven. It's my hope that I am forgiven for all the ways I've caused others harm too.

In life we're bound to encounter people who have different outlooks, different perspectives, different ways of interpreting experiences. Everyone has different ambitions, hopes, and dreams as well. In our family, we work hard to remember this. We all understand that we may not be the same or want the same things or believe the same things, but we can still be supportive of each other. I hope what I pass on to my kids is respect for another human being's choices for their own life as long as that choice is positive, helps others, or improves society.

In my family right now, several children are pursuing different things. They aren't too crazy about going into the brewing business. That's not a dream of theirs. They have their own paths to walk in life—real estate, fashion, horse jumping, polo, and acting, to name a few. They also have extremely different personalities and lifestyles. It's my job as a father to support and love them, not dictate what they should or shouldn't do. And their siblings don't have a say either. No one votes on what the other does. Rather, we are all there to support and encourage each other. They all know there isn't one Clydesdale to hitch your coach to in life. There are a lot of different horses to ride. There are lots of different paths to try. And there are a lot of different ways for people to grow and flourish.

For a long time, I thought my great-grandfather, grandfather, and father's legacy was brewing beer. But their true legacy, the one I will be passing on to my children, is, as trite as this sounds, to find your own path—make your own way. My great-grandfather left his homeland and his father's company and started his own here in America. My grand-father wanted to go West, and for a time he did. Though he ended up running the brewery, he did things his way every step of the way. He bought Grant's Farm and made it his sanctuary. He loved and adored his wife and family. My father did *everything* his own way—he carved new paths, over and over: building amusement parks, running a baseball team, and turning Budweiser into a global powerhouse. Each man had a dream for his life and was uncompromising in his pursuit of it. Sim-ilarly, I have my own path. And though among many dreams of mine is continuing the brewing legacy, my primary dream is to raise a family that is good to each other and that breaks the dysfunctional cycle that has endured for decades.

Another thing I inherited and hope to pass on to my children is the Busch resilience. Time after time, the Busch family was tested. We en-dured a lot of tragedy and setbacks, and every single time we rallied. We made it through hard times, heartbreaks, and disagreements before, and we have come out the other side wiser, stronger, and more determined than ever. I understand that everybody in my family is doing the best they can with what they've got and the tools they were given. Not ev-eryone had the same advantages or support. I was so fortunate to have found a woman like Christi to be my wife. We have each other's back. Not all my siblings have had such supportive spouses. I have also had my faith, which has sustained me through some of the darkest moments of my life. I have had the good fortune to read a lot of wonderful books that have helped me and guided me, and lastly, I have been able to grow up alongside my children. As most parents will tell you, children teach you more than you will ever teach them.

I also know I am constitutionally a positive, glass-half-full, everything-works-out-in-the-end, cockeyed optimist. I never shared in some of my siblings' bitterness or disappointment. Unlike some of them, I never expected anything to be handed to me—even Grant's Farm. I made the offer. It didn't work out. That's how things go. Instead of holding on to bitterness or hate, I just decided to let it all go and move on. Life doesn't give you much of a choice but to do so. Life keeps moving whether you like it or not. And though things didn't work out the way I'd hoped, I wish them all the best. I know this is an abundant world, and there is enough for everyone. We've all benefited such a great deal from our lives as Busches, and I, for one, am incredibly grateful for it.

My ultimate goal in writing this book was to tell my story—as I remember it. I am aware that my childhood is completely unique. There are not many children who have elephants as pets; private railcars, jets, and yachts; have the run of a baseball stadium; or live on the grounds of an amusement park. My siblings and I share not only the Busch name but a childhood wholly unlike anyone else's. It's true, we didn't always see eye to eye; over the years we have had our share of ups and downs, but in the end, I know that love remains. It always does.

I hope my children remember this one final note: I hope when they, like you, finish reading this book, they see that they have a choice to make every day. They can choose to continue a vicious cycle of dysfunction, or they can choose to stick together and put each other above all other things. I hope they remember that it's more important to understand each other than it is to compete with each other. I hope they've learned from my mistakes and the mistakes of my siblings, and I hope all who are reading this remember: When things get tough, go out, grab a beer, and talk through it. Listen to each other. And do whatever you have to do to move forward.

To my children specifically: My hope for all of you is simple. I hope you stay close to me, to Mom, and to each other for the rest of your lives. Nothing else is worth it. Not for all the riches in the world.

Acknowledgments

To my wife, Christi, who had the foresight to save boxes of memorabilia from my father and mother. Because of this, I was able to gather valuable insight into my great-grandparents, grandparents, and my dad in his younger days. Through all the trials and tribulations, you have stood by my side and helped me understand what's really important in life. Your intuition in knowing why I needed to write this book inspired me throughout the process. You are an amazing wife and mother, and I'm the luckiest husband in the world.

To John and Carol Myszak, Christi's parents, who set the example of what loving parents, grandparents, and in-laws look like. You have always been there for us.

I want to thank all my children—Billy, Haley, Abbey, Gussie, Gracie, Maddie, and Peter—who helped me recall some of the stories they remembered growing up and who listened intently to the stories I told them of the past. Take pride and inspiration in our legacy and learn from it. Words can't express the happiness you have brought me and how much I love you. Thank you for your patience and support throughout the journey of writing this book.

To Bill Volmer, the retired Anheuser-Busch historian, who may understand the history of Anheuser-Busch and the Busch family better than anyone alive today. Thank you for sharing your knowledge with me.

To Mary Curran Hackett for spending countless hours with me helping piece the book together.

Many thanks to my agent, Mel Berger at WME, who has always been a great support to my family and me.

To Blackstone Publishing who was passionate about my story being heard.

To Christina Boys and Kathryn Zentgraf the editors whose finishing touches reduced confusion and helped the book flow.

Last but not least, to my mom and dad. Through it all, you loved me and left me with incredible memories and values which I will always cherish. They inspire me to keep the family legacy and traditions alive, and to keep getting up no matter how often I get knocked down.

About the Author

Billy Busch was born and raised in St. Louis, Missouri, and still calls it home. He is the founder of the Busch Family Brewing & Distilling Company and an heir to the Anheuser-Busch multibillion-dollar fortune. He is the proud father of seven children and stars in the MTV reality series *The Busch Family Brewed*, which details life on their seven-hundred-acre estate as he and his wife, Christi, raise their children into hardworking and loving adults, despite all their wealth and privilege. Prior to the InBev takeover, Billy worked as a distributor and played professional polo. He was also the patron of the Bud Light polo team and winner of many tournaments, including the US Open. He is a graduate of St. Louis University and holds a bachelor's degree in psychology. He is married to Christi Busch, film producer, head of Busch Productions, and full-time *mom*ager of her seven children.